CRIME, PENAL POLICY AND SOCIAL WORK

by
Harry Blagg and **David Smith**

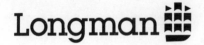
Longman

Longman Group UK Limited
The High, Westgate House,
Harlow, Essex CM20 1YR
Telephone (0279) 442601
Telex 81491 Padlog
Fax (0279) 444501

British Library Cataloguing in Publication Data
Crime, penal policy and social work.
  1. Great Britain. Welfare work with
  probationers.
  I. Smith, David, *1947 Aug 2-*   II. Blagg,
  Harry
  364.6'3'0941

ISBN 0-582-04792-7

0-582-04792-7

Typeset by Boldface Typesetters, London EC1.
Printed and bound in Great Britain by
Biddles Ltd, Guildford and King's Lynn

Contents

Acknowledgements   iv

Introduction   v

1   The influence of criminology on social policy and social work: *The uses of criminology; the labelling perspective; issues in policing; crime as reasoned action; masculinity, femininity and crime; conclusion.*   1

2   Managing the crisis: communities, crime and multi-agency work: *Broken windows; the law-and-order society; the racialisation of crime; re-focusing the crime debate; policing violence against women and children; responses to racism; working together; the limits and possibilities of multi-agency work.*   17

3   Problems of youth social work: themes and innovations: *The marginalization of youth – Case Study I: Midtown; Case Study II: Oldtown; a social approach to crime prevention – varieties of practice.*   46

4   Prisons and sentencing trends: *Numbers in the penal system; control, legitimacy and morale in prisons; sentencing patterns and 'alternatives' to custody.*   63

5   Developments in social work (i): Research and adult offenders: *Research developments – from outcomes to processes; monitoring the system; working with adult offenders – towards punishment in the community.*   83

6   Developments in social work (ii): Juvenile offenders: *The rise of the 'new orthodoxy'; cautioning and diversion; social inquiry reports; offending-focused work; social work and punishment in the community.*   99

7   Reparation, mediation and juvenile crime: philosophy and practice: *The critique of criminal justice; court-based and police-based models; Case Study I – Corby; Case Study II – Cumbria; conclusions.*   120

Conclusion: *social work and criminal justice.*   137

Bibliography   143

Acknowledgements

Many people have influenced our thinking on the issues discussed in this book. Some of our intellectual debts will be clear from the bibliography, but others will not, and we wish to acknowledge them here. We owe a particular debt to our co-workers in research into inter-agency co-operation in criminal justice, Geoffrey Pearson, Alice Sampson and Paul Stubbs. The research was funded by the ESRC (grant number EO 6250035), and we are grateful to the Council for its support. Conversations with Peter Raynor over many years have been a rich source of ideas. Alan Dearling at Longman has been helpful at all stages, from initial encouragement and planning to final editing. We are also indebted to many people in statutory and voluntary social and youth work agencies for putting up with our questions and sharing their experiences with us. We cannot list them all, but we should like to record particular debts to Gary Denman, Peter Dixon, Kevin Gill, Nigel Hinks, Dave Metcalfe, Mary Milton, Celia Moore and Jacky Smith. The faults of the book are of course entirely ours.

Introduction

The past twenty years have seen radical changes in the way in which crime and delinquency are understood, and in the efforts made to manage these forms of deviance. These changes have affected not only people who call themselves criminologists, but also people concerned with crime at a practical level, such as researchers and policy-makers in the various agencies which deal with crime and with those who commit it. Criminology as an academic discipline has changed almost beyond recognition, and ideas about what should be done about crime which were dominant in the 1960s now look to many people as antiquated as the biological theories advanced by Lombroso over a century ago. The image of the 'criminologist' as a detached, objective social scientist has become less plausible than ever; as the study of crime problems has become more closely related to questions of policy and practice, the boundary between criminology and social policy has grown increasingly blurred. While some purists in the academic community may regret this, we do not; our own work at Lancaster in some ways illustrates the process we have described, since it has involved us in action for change, as consultants, trainers and advisers, as well as in the more traditionally 'academic' pursuits. The tone and content of this book reflect our commitment to helping to bring about change in society's official responses to crime and delinquency.

At the same time, issues of crime and its control have become dramatically politicised: 'law and order' is now a major election issue, the work of the police is no longer taken for granted but is held up to political scrutiny, and social work agencies are increasingly being asked to behave in ways which many fear will make them less part of the welfare system and more part of the formal system of social control. In the background, there are the criminal statistics which seem to show a long-term trend for the volume of crime to increase (though not, as is sometimes believed, on a steady, year-by-year basis), and the statistics on the prison population, which show an apparently inexorable trend upwards, despite all efforts to reverse it.

With the emergence of law and order as a central political issue, criminology too has inevitably tended to become a more political affair; most writers no longer cling to the old ideal of lofty academic detachment (which does not mean that their arguments cannot be rationally evaluated). The focus of criminology has shifted from the criminal actor to the agencies of social control, and to those who are on the receiving end of crime, its victims. New areas for criminology have been opened out by writers concerned with issues of race and gender, and previously hidden or neglected topics have become matters of urgent debate: for example, the way the police deal with black people, both as (potential) offenders and as victims of racially motivated attacks, and with women and children who are victims of violence or sexual assault, particularly when this takes place in their own homes. The field has been politicised by the left as well as the right: while the traditional calls for more police with greater powers and for heavier sentences have been maintained, a very different agenda has emerged from the opposing camps, criticising the police for their lack of accountability, their racism and sexism, and their role as agents of government policy (a charge levelled particularly during the miners' strike).

The police themselves have not been as resistant to change or reluctant to listen to criticism as some pessimistic commentators predicted. It is now a commonplace among thoughtful police officers that the police cannot deal with crime problems alone, and that an increase in police powers or numbers is not the only way, and may not be the best, of reducing the incidence of crime. 'Community policing' in one form or another, which sounded a radical notion even ten years ago, is now widely practised and seen as an essential element of police practice, not as a luxury which could only be afforded in the leafy lanes of Devon. While community policing means a variety of things in practice, it always entails some stress on accessibility, accountability and co-operation both with the public and with other agencies. Reflecting a major shift in official thinking about the management of crime, community policing is also characterised by an interest in crime prevention rather than the detection of crimes already committed. Crime reduction has become a central theme not only of explicitly law-and-order policies but also of policies in housing, education and social work.

Social work and youth work agencies are increasingly expected to be involved in the crime reduction enterprise, and to see their work in preventive as well as reactive terms. That is, they are not to work towards the reform or 'cure' of individual offenders, or even simply to help and support them, in isolation from other agencies; they are to remember that they are a part of a wider system that includes all the agencies concerned with crime and its control. This view of the purposes of social work and the place of welfare within criminal justice is uncomfortable for many practitioners, but it can be seen as, in part, a logical development from trends within social work practice. In the 1970s it became difficult for social workers to justify their involvement in the system in the terms they had traditionally used – that they were experts in the diagnosis and treatment of the sickness that caused crime. But if this 'treatment model' could not be rationally defended, what justification was there for a social work presence in the system? In our view, social workers have come up with some successful answers to this question, but there remains a good deal of unease and uncertainty about the place of social work in criminal justice, especially in the probation service. Morale is not helped by the increasingly less veiled threat that private enterprise may be encouraged to become involved in the control and surveillance of offenders.

The aim of this book is to describe and discuss the changes outlined above in a way that is accessible and useful to practitioners and managers in social work and related agencies. Chapter 1 sketches some recent changes in criminology which we think are relevant to social workers, and which have influenced thinking and practice in official agencies, especially the police. Chapter 2 broadens the focus, and attempts to place the changes in criminology in a historical and political context. We deal here with the political shifts which many have argued represent a move towards a more authoritarian state, and with the impact they have had on the social control of those officially defined as deviant or dangerous. We criticise the ideological approach of 'Thatcherism' to issues of crime and social order, and argue that the Conservative attack on welfare institutions has generated resistance and opposition. This is explored through more detailed discussion of issues of race and racism and of violence against women in the home, and of how the much canvassed 'solution' of inter-agency co-operation works out in practice in the urban areas in which crime problems are seen as being most pressing.

Chapter 3 gives an account, based on research, of how social workers and youth workers have responded to the problems discussed theoretically in the previous chapter. Following a recent trend, we call their practice 'youth social work', and show the wide range of activities this term covers. This chapter introduces a recurring theme: our wish to support forms of preventive work which are social and developmental rather than purely situational and negative. Chapter 4 shifts the focus to a discussion of the problems of the prison system, which is intended to provide a backdrop to the next three chapters. The size of the prison population has been at the heart of penal policy and criminal justice legislation for more than twenty years. We try to show that overcrowding is only one of the problems the prison system faces, and discuss sentencing trends and the fate of 'alternatives' to custody in a way which we hope is rationally critical without being over-pessimistic.

Chapters 5 and 6 deal with the ways in which social work, defined more narrowly, has responded to official injunctions to play a central part in the reduction of the prison population, and in the management of deviant youth. Chapter 5 reviews the research findings from which the conclusion was drawn in the 1970s that 'nothing works', and traces the movement away from a focus on individual offenders towards an interest in system intervention and change as the main purpose of social work involvement in criminal justice. It then moves to a discussion of developments in work with adult offenders; the emphasis is on the probation service, although it is clear that it cannot be usefully discussed in isolation from developments in other agencies. Chapter 6 concentrates on recent trends in social work with juvenile offenders; we must admit that for us 'IT' still means Intermediate Treatment (whatever that is), and not Information Technology. The chapter concludes with an analysis of the present debates about 'punishment in the community' and the relevance of experience of work with juveniles to work with young adults.

Chapter 7 again draws on research to explore the problems and possibilities of various forms of mediation and reparation in criminal justice. The chapter takes a more sceptical view than some enthusiasts, but is less sceptical about the value of this type of work than some of its critics. The brief concluding chapter tries to summarise the major themes of the book in a way which does not deny the problems raised for social workers by critical theoretical analysis, but does not succumb to a paralysing gloom.

A word about terminology, and an apology. (1) 'Social work' and 'social workers' may be assumed to include the probation service and probation officers, and voluntary as well as statutory agencies and their workers, unless the context makes clear that a distinction is being made. (2) Scotland appears erratically in our discussions, and Northern Ireland not at all. Welsh readers may also wonder about the entity 'England and Wales'. We regret the omissions and the tendency for our discussion to concentrate on events south of Hadrian's Wall and east of Offa's Dyke. It arises from a reliance on the most accessible official figures and on books with the same geographical limitation; but we wish we were less ignorant.

1 The influence of criminology on social policy and social work

In this chapter we want to show how developments in criminology over the past twenty years have been reflected in developments in social policy and practice. Some people, including some criminologists, might be surprised by the claim implicit in that sentence – that criminology has had an influence. We hope to show that it has, at any rate if one takes a fairly broad view of what counts as criminology; and we shall argue that only a broad view makes sense, since the field has become increasingly diffuse. Efforts to define criminology prescriptively – as the sociology of deviance, for example, or the scientific study of the criminal mind – are in our view misguided and unhelpful; the diversity of criminological writing may make for untidiness, but it is also a sign of life. We think that in fact some clear trends have emerged from the apparent muddle in the last ten years particularly, and that these have made criminology more relevant and useful to practitioners than before.

The uses of criminology

In a way it seems odd that the relevance of criminology has ever been an issue – not just whether it is influential on policy and practice, but whether it should be. Criminology, it seems to us, is by definition an applied discipline; its bounds are set by the criminal law, and perhaps by other sets of social rules and norms; and in studying law- and rule-breaking, and what is or should be done with the people involved, it is concerned with issues which are defined, by a rough consensus, as social problems, not just sociological problems. It is unhelpful and unrealistic, then, to pretend that the subject-matter of criminology has no implications beyond the boundaries of academic theorising; as Downes and Rock (1988) remark, 'all theories of deviance have implications for policy'. This wider relevance was assumed by the writers who established criminology as a distinct area of study. It is equally true of Lombroso, for example, whose theories of biological atavism in criminals may look quaint and nasty now, but were extremely influential around the turn of the century, and of the pioneering sociologists of the Chicago School, who saw the city both as a 'laboratory' in which social life could be minutely studied and as a place actually inhabited by people who experienced problems which sociology could identify and try to resolve.

The idea that criminology positively ought not to have any policy relevance is a comparatively recent one, and it may be that its influence will prove short-lived. The idea, in Britain at least, can be mainly attributed to the 'new criminologists' who became influential in the early 1970s (Taylor, Walton and Young, 1973; 1975). What was 'new' about their criminology was essentially the attempt to apply some orthodox Marxist tenets to the sociology of deviance. Previous writers were in varying degrees criticised for their failure to be Marxist enough, and it was argued that to be truly radical the new criminologist must remain aloof from current issues of policy, since to do other than hasten the collapse of capitalism would be to compromise with the 'correctionalism' of a repressive system. The pressing tasks for radical criminology were seen as theoretical rather than empirical – a position which threatened to leave the new criminologists with no-one to talk to except themselves. The difficulties of this stance have since been recognised by some erstwhile 'new criminologists'; instead of priding themselves on the principled irrelevance of their work, they have begun to try to bring criminology back into some contact with the world most of us live in. This has entailed the development of a 'left realism' (as opposed to 'left idealism'), in the work of Taylor (1981) and in particular of the group of criminologists associated with Jock Young at Middlesex Polytechnic (e.g. Lea and Young, 1984; Matthews and Young, 1986). In common with other writers, we have serious reservations about some of the tenets of 'left realism' (Smith, 1984), but we at least agree that criminology ought to have something to do with the issues of crime and its control which are of immediate public and political concern. To clarify, we ought to add that there are radical criminologists (for example, Scraton, 1987) who have never thought otherwise; it is in fact possible to be both radical and relevant.

We assume, then, that criminology can and should address issues that are relevant to policy-makers and practitioners. A further point is that the present policy context is one which may well seem likely to be especially hospitable to criminological ideas. It is possible to detect in many policy fields a process which can be called a 'criminalisation' of the discourses of social policy (Blagg *et al*, 1988; Pearson, 1983). By this we mean that the justification for policy initiatives is increasingly presented in terms of their potential to control or reduce crime.

This applies, for example, to architecture, town planning, environmental improvement and the design of housing estates; to concerns
about discipline in schools and the content of curricula; to job
creation and training schemes; to youth work and community development; and to social work in child care as well as in more obvious
fields such as probation. This is not solely a British trend (Hope and
Shaw, 1988), but there is a peculiarly British slant to it, because of
the prominence of law and order as a political issue and the tendency
of some Conservative politicians to blame liberal or 'permissive'
influences in social policy for many things, and for crime and disorder in particular.

In this context, criminology ought to be able to exercise some
influence. Some commentators have placed their emphasis on how
little has in practice been achieved (e.g. Downes and Rock, 1988).
They suggest a number of reasons: theorists may not be interested in
practical applications of their work; they may lack the energy or the
talent for political struggle; their concepts may not be readily trans-
latable into the everyday concerns of policy-making, and so on.
Downes and Rock remark that it is harder to do something about
'anomie' than to tackle vandalism by technical means (shatter-proof
glass or climb-proof drainpipes). We agree; but the task is not impossible. Some of the attempts at 'social' crime prevention which we discuss later have something very like the reduction of anomie as their
aim, and certainly the French projects described by Michael King
(1988) are not afraid to say so. Furthermore, it is not as clear as might
be expected that straightforward technical 'fixes' actually work
better than the more ambitious and wide-ranging efforts to reduce
crime by (say) reducing anomie. So our emphasis is rather different.
We are more struck by the uses to which criminological theory is put
in practice than by its absence. We recognise that the influence of
theory and research on policy and practice is often indirect and
dependent on contingent factors, such as the political salience a problem has or acquires at a given time; Rock (1986) provides a good
account of the process of influence in his case study of a Canadian
initiative on victims. But this is not surprising; certainly it will not be
news to practitioners or their managers. It may be a special academic
naïvety to expect policy to be formed solely on the basis of rational
consideration of research findings or theoretical insights.

What are the criminological theories which have been influential,
and how is their influence shown? To answer these questions we
need first to give a brief outline of what has happened to criminology
in the past two decades. This is in no way an attempt to provide a
complete history; readers who are interested in this should go to the
special issue of the *British Journal of Criminology* of Spring 1988 (now
reprinted in book form), which brought together a wide range of con-
tributors to provide a rich account from the inside of the development

of British criminology. Our brief sketch is indebted to this collection, but we want to highlight the developments which seem to us particularly relevant to our concerns with policy and practice.

One thing which emerges clearly from the *British Journal*'s history is how recent the appearance of something recognisable as criminology has been. In particular, sociological approaches have been with us for little more than thirty years. For instance, Martin (1988) describes Terence Morris's 1957 study of *The Criminal Area* as 'the first home grown sociological study' – though we think that Mays (1954) might claim priority. 'Home grown', because not American, but Morris inevitably drew on American studies, particularly on work in the Chicago tradition: his focus was on a small area (in Croydon); he used ecological concepts to describe its peculiarities; and he was interested in the policy implications (as was Mays). Martin argues that criminology in the period covered by his essay, 1948–60, was barely influenced by the developing American sociology of deviance; that began to take hold in the 1960s. But he does show clearly that there was a shift towards more sociologically inclined interpretations, and away from the medical/psychiatric model which was dominant immediately after the war. He concludes that:

> The foremost intellectual achievement of the period was probably the cutting down to size of the psycho-analytical approach to criminology. The *coup de grâce* was delivered by Barbara Wootton in *Social Science and Social Pathology* (p 44).

Wootton's book was also instrumental in reducing, though not removing, the influence of psychoanalytic thinking in social work. We shall return to the question of how great this influence was on practice, but there is no doubt that the psychoanalytically based work of John Bowlby, for instance, was important in shaping the development of post-war policies in child care. It also shows the close link there has traditionally been between child care policies and the concern with delinquency; the 'criminalisation' of policy we referred to above is not a new phenomenon.

The essay following Martin's has to cover a great deal of ground. Downes' (1988) title is 'The sociology of crime and social control in Britain 1960–1987', and we think his inclusion of 'social control' in the review is significant. If we were asked to give a single example of a criminological approach which has influenced policy and practice in the provision of services to offenders we should point to the labelling perspective. Its influence within criminology has been equally decisive, in shifting attention away from the criminal actor and on to those who label and define his or (much more rarely) her criminality – in particular, the official agencies which are responsible for the regulation and management of deviance and the deviant. Downes suggests that there have been losses as well as gains in the wake of the success of the labelling perspective. For instance, 'good ethnography is now in especially short supply'; one of the central streams of work in the sociology of deviance since the days of the Chicago School may be in danger of drying up. Downes remarks that out of 147 research proposals made in response to a recent initiative by the Economic and Social Research Council only three were concerned with inner city crime; perhaps it is thought that we already know all that is to be known about this. Instead, the emphasis has shifted towards questions of policing, new varieties of 'control theory', and studies of 'penality' and the criminal justice system. That is, it has shifted away from the questions about criminals – who they are, what they do, and particularly what makes them do it – which were the main focus of the old 'positivist' tradition.

These research areas by no means exhaust the field; Downes also lists as recently developed fields of study victimisation, the political manifestations of 'law and order', gender issues in crime and criminal justice, and the 'left realist' agenda of taking public worries about crime seriously. But these themes, too, represent a change of direction, in that they either deal directly with policy issues or open out new areas for study, such as domestic violence and the fear of crime. There is something of a paradox here. The labelling perspective appealed to many radically inclined young sociologists of deviance in the late 1960s because it seemed to challenge the traditional correctional thrust of criminology and to encourage identification with the deviants rather than with their would-be controllers (Pearson, 1975). But it also encouraged interest in what the social control agencies were doing, and, combined with a certain amount of pragmatism and a revived sense that reform this side of revolution may still be worth having, this can reunite criminologists with policy concerns.

The labelling perspective

If, with Becker (1963), you were on the side of the underdog (and it was difficult not to side with his marijuana-using jazz musicians against the drugs squad), you had some obligation to think about what would improve the underdog's lot; and the labelling perspective quite readily generated explicit policy prescriptions – non-intervention (radical or otherwise), destigmatisation, decriminalisation, diversion from official agencies, decarceration and so on, all strongly influential on the thinking and practice of social, youth and community workers in the 1970s and 80s. The process has been noted by Heidensohn (1988) among others; she writes that 'the area will never be the same again' following the impact of 'new deviancy' perspectives, and notes that the key terms of the 'new deviancy' theorists are now 'commonplace discourse in social work text books ... and in the practice and making of penal policies and treatment philosophies' (pp 81–2). There is a faint air of surprise about this, as if the theorists never expected that anyone outside academic criminology would actually listen to them, let alone try to put into practice the implications of their message. But if criminology is and should be an applied discipline, there is nothing surprising about it. Since it is impossible to do everything at once, and since, as Rock (1988) notes, the number of 'pure' criminologists is declining along with the funding to support them, it is inevitable that some areas of study will be neglected. The expectation that academic institutions should become more self-supporting financially is also bound to encourage applied, policy-oriented research at the expense of work without obvious utility. This is, of course, a sign of the times, and we regret that knowledge 'for its own sake' (which in fact often turns out to have unanticipated implications for policy) is no longer seen as worthy of support. As impure criminologists, however, we regard the changes over the past ten years or so as generally positive: they represent the return to criminology of a sense of relevance, and of the centrality both of policies and politics, which in our view is essential to its continuing health.

The policy prescriptions which were derived from the labelling perspective have by now quite a long history in British penal policy and practice, although, as we shall see, their implementation has not always produced the results which were intended. The 1969 Children and Young Persons Act, for example, was clearly decriminalising and diversionary in intent, and over the subsequent decade what had seemed a radical policy recommendation – 'Leave the kids alone' (if you possibly can) – became part of the established orthodoxy in thinking about juvenile offenders, reflected in White Papers and Home Office circulars encouraging the use of cautions rather than prosecutions as well as in the practice of social workers and probation officers. The 'decarceration' message has also been reflected in policy, though with discouraging results; nevertheless, there is now a broad consensus that there should be fewer people in prison, even if policies towards this end have not been as vigorous as many would have liked, and it remains uncertain, to put it no higher, how this aim can be achieved.

Indeed, there is irony in the fact that while the policy implications of the labelling perspective and other critical analyses of the social control apparatus have influenced the thinking of people working at all levels within the system, the results tend to be discouraging. Stanley Cohen's *Visions of Social Control* (1985), a deserved instant classic in the field, has as its core theme the failure of liberal attempts at reform. There is a tension in the book, which Cohen explores in his final chapter, between the sociologist as a detached, critical, adversarial observer and the sociologist as an activist, involved in trying to explore ways in which past failures might be avoided in the future.

Cohen tells us that 'aesthetically' he is drawn to the traditional view of the sociologist as a privileged academic, who should resist becoming involved in the design of technical fixes for the social control system. But he came to sociology *via* social work, and retains a concern with private troubles as well as with public issues; unlike some writers in the field, he actually knows about social work and social workers. To his credit, he also sees it as 'a simple matter of intellectual integrity and honesty to clarify the policy implications of social-problem analysis' (p 238). This entails a difficult coming to terms with the mostly pessimistic implications of his account while trying to avoid foreclosing all possibilities of constructive change.

Cohen suggests that if we think about the original values that lay behind the reforming movements which drew on the labelling perspective we have a choice: either explicitly to abandon them or 'cautiously' to reaffirm them. He chooses, fortunately, the second option, so that for him it still makes 'some sense' to look for more constructive alternatives to prison, to defend the values of 'community', to be critical of centralised, professionalised and bureaucratic solutions, to seek to integrate deviant groups rather than exclude them, and to try to limit the 'seemingly inexorable' process of increased classification and control. Thus he tries to extract some hope from his gloomy visions (not that his tone is gloomy: it is spirited and combative), and to address short-term possibilities – the sort of choices that daily confront social work practitioners and managers – as well as long-term goals of global change.

Our own view is that Cohen is more pessimistic than he need be, perhaps because of a tendency to conflate American with British experience: there really is a problem of translatability here, because the American (US) experience of crime is in many ways exceptional, not least because of the sheer volume of it. Unfortunately, it is not only British criminologists who sometimes seem to be hypnotised by American writing and research on crime and crime control: there are recent signs that the same applies to politicians and national policy-makers: how else to explain the recent fascination with 'tracking' and electronic 'tagging' – the latter, incidentally, far less central to American systems of surveillance than those in charge at the Home Office seem to imagine? Cohen's overall pessimism may turn out to be justified; we hope not, and later in the book offer some arguments and evidence in support of a cautious optimism. But it does have to be acknowledged that an analysis like Cohen's more readily generates pessimism than optimism: his picture of a deviancy control system that continually expands to classify and regulate new groups, widening the net, thinning the mesh, and 'penetrating' communities ever more deeply, bears an unmistakable likeness to what is actually going on. The problem for social workers is how to take the implications of the analysis without being paralysed by it, or plunged into terminal gloom.

Policing

Social workers, excessively given to public breast-beating and private agonising over their failures and inadequacies, might take grim consolation from contemplating the difficulties of the agency which is most clearly central to the enterprise of deviancy control, the police. One of the products of the transformation of the field of criminology by the labelling perspective was, as we noted above, a new critical interest in police policy and practice. The police have in the past ten years come under unprecedented scrutiny both from academic researchers and from local political and interest groups concerned with the issues of accountability and priorities in local police practice. The reaction of the police is often highly defensive; they have not been used to this kind of critical exposure. On the other hand, we think that there are instances where the police have made a serious effort to improve their work, in response to identification of their failings either by outside critics or internally. We want to review briefly some relevant issues that have emerged from recent studies of the police, and indicate how rational preferences between policing practices might be worked out.

There has been so much recent work on the police that our account of it is necessarily highly selective; there are guides to the literature in Reiner (1985) and Reiner and Shapland (1987). The range includes technical evaluations, observational and ethnographic studies, historical accounts, and critical analyses of the political role of the police and the 'militarisation' of police practice. The policing of the riots in 1981 and 1985, and of the miners' strike, brought the last-mentioned issues into public prominence, producing widespread political and media concern as well as attacks from radical academics (Scraton, 1985; Fine and Millar, 1986). As Reiner (1985) put it, the public image of the police was becoming less like Dixon of Dock Green and more like Darth Vader; and it seemed to many commentators that a paramilitary national police force had in fact developed, despite the supposed British tradition that rejected such a force. In some areas at least it was no longer plausible to argue that the police operated with the consent, let alone the active support, of local people; and there was particularly clear evidence of a breakdown in relations between the police and black people, especially the young. Two major inquiries into the origins of the riots found that police action had been initially important in turning resentment and suspicion into violent confrontation (Scarman, 1981; Gifford, 1986).

At a more mundane level, a number of studies have been critical of police attitudes and behaviour, and have illuminated the apparently routine racism and sexism of the police's occupational culture (Smith and Gray, 1983; Jones, 1986). Evaluation studies by the Home Office Research and Planning Unit and others have cast doubt on police claims that their effectiveness (in terms of the crimes cleared up) would be greatly increased by more resources, in the form of more officers or still more advanced technology. Clarke and Hough (1984), for example, point out that most detective work is very different from the fictional images of it, being either straightforward, when the offender's identity is obvious from the start, or almost hopeless. The police have been criticised for their excessive and unrealistic reliance on technology (Hough, 1985), and critics have noted the rapid escalation in policing costs, unaccompanied by any clear evidence of improved performance. Heal *et al* (1985) observe that expenditure on policing increased by 280 % between 1977 and 1986, faster than spending on defence and social security, and almost three times as fast as spending on education. On the other hand, efforts to develop a lower-key, more community-oriented style of policing have also been criticised. Weatheritt (1986) casts doubt on the claims made for crime prevention initiatives and community policing, suggesting that what little research has been done is not very encouraging, and that the enthusiasm for these activities is based on faith rather than reason. More radical critics, such as Gordon (1984), dismiss community policing as a front behind which the local police state can be set up. And while studies continue to suggest a fairly high level of public satisfaction with the police, there is evidence that this level has declined over the past twenty years or so, and that satisfaction varies between social groups. It is hardly surprising that levels of satisfaction are highest among the white middle class in rural areas, and lowest among the black working class in inner cities (Southgate and Ekblom, 1985).

The explosion of research on the police in the past ten years, then, is liable to make the police feel somewhat threatened and even beleaguered. Insofar as social workers and other groups with whom the police are expected to work are aware of the research (and they will certainly be aware of the spectacular instances of breakdown in police–public relations), they are likely to feel more suspicious about co-operation with the police, and less confident about its value. In a later chapter we explore some issues arising from our research on inter-agency co-operation of the kind that is often recommended in official guidance to the police and other agencies, and suggest that it is neither the panacea it is sometimes presented as being, nor a sinister fulfilment of prophecies of an ever-tighter web of social control. For the present, we want to indicate what in our view the research suggests about possible improvements in policing practice. We think that, despite the defensiveness they often display in the face of criticism and even of comment, the police are more capable of taking criticism seriously and trying to respond to it than some pessimistic accounts suggest (e.g. Scraton, 1985). Paradoxically, the Metropolitan police, which of all the forces is the least subject to any form of democratic accountability, may feel under more pressure than most to respond, because the politicisation of policing has been taken further in London than almost anywhere else. We think policing should be a political question, and that the irritation the Metropolitan police doubtless felt when the GLC began to make it one (Christian, 1983) has been justified by subsequent action. The police in London, for example, have in the last three years adopted policies which give much higher priority than before to incidents of domestic violence and to racial attacks. We do not know how these policies are working out in practice, but it surely counts as a progressive move that such policies exist.

We assume, then, that the police are capable of being influenced by both academic research and political argument – and we should remember that the police force is not a monolithic institution: it contains a diversity of views and some capacity to tolerate them; and struggles for influence go on within it, just as they do within a social services department. Broadly speaking, we think that social workers and other professional groups which come into contact with the police should support tendencies towards greater accountability (while recognising that police officers must have room to exercise discretion on the street), greater accessibility, and, in line with the suggestions of Shapland and Vagg (1987), a greater willingness to share power and 'ownership' of problems of crime and disorder with members of the lay public. In terms of relations between the police and other agencies, one positive effect of recent research has been to make clear that problems of crime cannot be resolved by the police alone. This is not in our view just a 'cop-out' but a recognition of reality; and it should, and on occasions does, mean that the police are prepared to share power with agencies whose structural position tends to make them subordinate. An example of this is the investigation of alleged child sexual abuse, which in some areas at least is a genuinely co-operative enterprise in which women police officers work alongside women social workers.

To sum up, we think that there are some detectable trends in policing which are preferable to others. At the most general level, we want to support the concept of community policing that attempts to respond locally and to take seriously the problems of sections of the population, particularly women and black people, who have often been neglected in policing priorities. This is certainly preferable to any further militarisation of policing. Our preference will not surprise many readers; but it is worth emphasising that we have reached it in full awareness of the political objections that many on the left have raised to community policing. It is also the preference that in our view is best supported by the evaluation research. While it is no doubt true, as Weatheritt (1986) argues, that there is little convincing research evidence for the effectiveness of community policing in crime control, the thrust of most recent research has been that there is equally little evidence for the effectiveness of other approaches. Clarke and Hough (1987 took the view that while the police have an impact on levels of crime (without any police, we would expect crime rates to be higher), there was 'only limited scope' for enhancing this impact. If this is so, we should prefer policing styles that are open, accessible and responsive rather than secretive and alienating; and we should think of the aims of policing in broader terms than a straight-forward crime control function. For example, reducing fear of crime where this fear is irrational or exaggerated might be a reasonable aim (though we recognise that some fear of crime is rational and justi-fied); and the growth of interest in recent years in the experience of victimisation suggests a role for the police in supporting and giving helpful information to victims. These aims are more compatible with the principles and methods of community policing than with para-militarism.

Crime as reasoned action

We want to return now to another aspect of recent criminology which we think is especially relevant to the themes of this book. This is the revival in recent years of a version of 'control theory'. 'Control theory', very broadly, refers to a body of criminological thought which starts with the assumption that people commit crimes when the controls that most of us usually feel as restraints upon deviant behaviour are (perhaps temporarily) absent or weakened. Although control theory can be traced back to one of the founders of sociology, Emile Durkheim, it has not, as Downes and Rock (1988) remark, enjoyed much of a following among sociologists until recently, per-haps because it looks too much like common sense, and sociologists would rather surprise us with the unexpected. Nevertheless, some very influential sociologists of deviance have drawn on control theory, including David Matza (1964), with his account of the 'drift' into delinquency in the juvenile gang, equipped with 'techniques of neutralisation' which free its members from the bonds of morality; Travis Hirschi (1969), who employed a much more thorough-going version of the theory to explore the causes of delinquency in terms of lack of attachment to others; and (a British example) Steven Box (1981), who sought to combine control theory with the labelling per-spective to explain why, while self-report studies show weak links between social class, race and delinquency, official statistics show very strong links.

We do not intend to review here the merits or failings of different forms of control theory; instead we shall briefly note that what has seemed a weakness to some sociologists – their resemblance to common sense – seems to us a strength; it has certainly allowed control theories such as Hirschi's and especially Matza's to be directly influential on social work practice (Thorpe *et al*, 1980). Our primary interest, however, is in the recent impact of control theories on social and penal policy. This is sometimes assumed to be inevitably negative and repressive, and there is a tendency for those who espouse control theories to identify with Conservative, anti-welfarist positions in penal policy. Wilson (1975), for example, writing in the context of the apparent failure of attempts to rehabilitate or reform offenders, argued that the only sure way of reducing crime was to incapacitate those likely to commit it – that is, they should be locked up, preferably for a long time. It is true that the revival of interest in control theory is associated with the decline in belief in rehabilitation, and indeed with a loss of faith in the ability of criminology to explain crime in any but commonsensical terms. But in our view this does not inevitably mean that its social policy implications are of a traditionally repressive, conservative kind, although we must acknowledge that such implications could be drawn.

A central element of much control theory (Hirschi's, for example), is that offences should be seen as the product of some kind of reasoning process (Cornish and Clarke, 1986). The offender is someone who decides to commit an offence, and may therefore equally decide not to. A number of possible lines of social policy flow from this. One which we explore in detail later is that social work practice which aims to reduce people's propensity to offend should attend to their reasoning processes, in particular those that are relevant to offending. This form of cognitively oriented social work, concerned with helping people think more clearly about their problems, and make more rational choices on the basis of a better understanding, is, as we shall, see, increasingly influential, and we regard its influence as positive (Priestley *et al*, 1977; Denman, 1982). But another line of policy thinking, the influence of which is perhaps more obvious, runs as follows: since we do not know what dispositional factors make some people more likely to commit crimes than others, and even if we did, we could not affect them, it makes sense to see crime more as a product of opportunity than of disposition. The most promising approach to crime control is therefore to reduce opportunities for crimes to be committed with a reasonable prospect, from the offender's point of view, of success. This 'crime as opportunity' thesis is in agreement with the idea that the offender is rational and calculating, and leads to efforts to change not the offender but the environment. In particular, it is associated with what is conventionally known as 'situational' crime prevention.

This approach has been closely linked in Britain with the work of the Home Office Crime Prevention Unit, established in 1983. Ronald Clarke, who had previously conducted research, with discouraging results, on the effects of a residential treatment on delinquency, was instrumental in the founding of the Unit, and his own career encapsulates the general trend away from rehabilitative optimism towards pessimism – at least about changing offenders. It might, however, be possible to remain optimistic about changing the environment, characteristically through increasing security or intensifying surveillance, or by some combination of the two. Thus the approach can encompass a wide range of initiatives, from 'target-hardening' by means of burglar alarms, entryphones, strengthened doors and the like, to Neighbourhood Watch, which may be attractive as a means both of increasing surveillance and of generating community spirit and involvement (another instance of the 'criminalisation' of social policy).

Advocates of this approach can claim some successes; for instance, an experimental property-marking in South Wales reduced domestic burglaries (Laycock, 1985); and the approach seems to be in line with what burglars actually think about when they are contemplating a burglary (Bennett and Wright, 1984). On the other hand, there have been some failures, mainly resulting from problems of implementation (Hope, 1984); and the success of Neighbourhood Watch schemes, which are much better established in the United States than in Britain, is disputed (Rosenbaum, 1988), although enthusiasts continue to make high claims for them. Beyond these technical issues, the approach raises political questions which in our view ought to temper the enthusiasm for it. It very readily conjures up a vision of a paranoid fortress society – one in which, moreover, crime prevention is structured along lines of class and wealth, with those who can afford crime prevention measures living in relative security, while those who cannot are left unprotected, the weak preying upon the weakest. This grim vision has informed some excellent fictional accounts, notably Pete Davies' *The Last Election*; a less lurid version of it seems to be increasingly influential in policy-making circles, leading to a recognition that purely situational measures may lead to injustice and repression if they are not accompanied by more socially oriented approaches (Hope and Shaw, 1988). We think this policy shift is in line with the broad implications of control theories.

For example, control theorists have emphasised that young offenders tend to lack motivation and aspiration, often as a result of school failure or lack of parental interest; and their low level of commitment to conventional lines of behaviour, to use Hirschi's terms, may realistically reflect their prospects in the employment market. It is thus a mistake simply to read off from control theories a set of prescriptions for tougher sentencing, heavier surveillance and the like. Their broad social policy implications are essentially the same as those

traditionally derived from 'strain' theories, which directly emphasise
class inequalities in education, environment, culture and employment. Control theories, despite their association with rehabilitative
despair, are quite compatible with the advocacy of reformist, redis-
tributive social policies. This is not the way in which they are most
obviously used by the present government, but it is certainly one way
in which they could be used. We explore the possibilities in depth
later, when discussing efforts in social crime prevention.

Masculinity, femininity and crime

There is a connection between control theories and the final aspect of
recent criminology which we wish to stress – the concern with
women both as offenders and as victims. It ought to be an axiom in
evaluating any criminological theory that it should give an adequate
account of the differences in offending between males and females.
Sex is after all the best single variable as a predictor of crime. Yet
until recently criminology barely attended to this question; the
higher propensity of males of all ages to offend was simply assumed.
Control theorists have been as culpable in this respect as members of
rival schools of explanation, but control theory may be better able
than others to accommodate an explanation of why girls and women
are so much more conforming than boys and men.

Heidensohn (1985; 1988) argues that the most striking feature of
the process of socialisation into the feminine role is its success in
achieving a high level of conformity among girls and women, and
that this has potentially far-reaching implications for male crime and
masculinity. Masculine and macho values have been recognised by
some commentators, for instance on youth subcultures, as important
variables, but generally the implications of this for policy have not
been followed through; the same should be said about the identification of the power of the same values in studies of the police. One
problem has been the tendency of some male writers to admire and
even identify with these characteristics of their research subjects
(male academics doing research on the police seem particularly prone
to this). On the other hand, some writers, such as Willis (1977) have
observed the limiting and constricting effect of masculine values on
working-class youth, and the policy-sensitive work of the Football
Research Centre at Leicester University has also emphasised the
importance of these values in shaping the preoccupations of football
'hooligans' with territoriality and aggression (Dunning, Murphy and
Williams, 1987). There are signs, then, that the importance of sex
and gender roles in crime is beginning to be recognised in a way that
may influence future policy initiatives.

How far might these be taken? Heidensohn (1988) asks why
societies tolerate as they do the costs of 'masculine' behaviour, and

suggests that solutions to crime might be found in socialising boys and young men in the way that girls and young women are now socialised; if this entails some restriction on their public freedom, well, such restrictions have long been judged acceptable for girls. She invites us to ponder the irony that whenever there is a horrific rape or sexual murder the police advise women to stay indoors, when it would be 'at least as rational to keep all men under curfew' (p 110). The reaction of many men, of course, will be that this would represent a repressive restriction of civil liberties; but it is no different from the restriction on the freedom of women which is now imposed as a matter of routine. At the very least, the insights of recent feminist criminology should make us think about the possibilities of 'feminising' the socialisation of boys, and developing for boys the kind of informal mechanisms of social control which seem to work well for girls. The policy and practice implications of this have hardly begun to be explored, but some are obvious. For instance, it does not make much sense to sentence boys and young men to prisons which explicitly emphasise masculine values in the toughness and authoritarian style of their regimes; and the attempts which are now being made in some social work with offenders to challenge sexist attitudes and discourage traditional masculine responses to problems should not be regarded as optional extras or as cosmetic gestures. They may be the most important elements of the work.

Conclusion

In this chapter we have, in a sketchy and highly selective way, tried to show how recent developments in criminology may be relevant to the questions of policy and practice in criminal justice. We have on the whole taken an optimistic view of the possible usefulness of criminology, although this will not take the form that early criminologists would have wished. That is, social workers should not look to criminology (perhaps they never did) for an answer to the question: What causes this person to behave in this way, and what should I do about it? The answers were never very helpful (psychoanalysis, referral to a psychologist, do nothing, overthrow the capitalist system), and criminologists have, quite rightly, stopped trying to provide them. What social workers can gain from criminology is a number of insights into the nature of the practice of their own agencies, and the ways in which this may have unanticipated, latent and undesired consequences. They can gain ideas and information about the practices of other agencies, especially the police, and some basis for a critical understanding of how and why they might wish to co-operate with police activities. They can find a range of ideas on crime prevention and a lively debate, still unresolved, about what approaches are likely to prove progressive and effective. In the image of the reasoning criminal, they can find a much more accessible and helpful basis for relevant practice than the old paradigm of psychoanalysis ever provided. Finally, they can find a powerful new line of thinking which stresses the crucial importance of sex and gender in understanding and responding to crime. In sum, this is not the answer to every social worker's prayer, but it is not something social workers can afford to ignore either; and there is of course much in recent criminology that we have not discussed.

In the rest of this book, we explore in greater depth how these themes in the study of crime and social control are or could be reflected in the practices of the welfare agencies concerned with crime and offenders, and with the consequences of crime for others. In the next chapter, we discuss further some of the areas of study opened up by recent criminology, and set them in the context of a wider analysis of the social and political changes which have affected official and other conceptions of crime and its control.

2 Managing the crisis: communities, crime and multi-agency work

The belief that 'crime' undermines community and neighbourhood integration is one that has taken root in official and some academic thinking. In the 1960s there was a concern that poverty and deprivation similarly threatened the fabric of communities and social networks. The answer then was to strengthen community networks by building support structures within communities, through which the disadvantaged could 'mobilise' themselves, although cynics argued that this was just a means whereby the 'ghetto' could be 'gilded' (Community Development Projects, 1977), and the 'disinherited' 'neutralised' (Rainwater, 1978).

Since the 1970s, however, this concern with deprivation has given way to an emphasis on criminality and deviance as the major problem faced by communities. Intervention in order to protect and support neighbourhoods and localities, which previously could have been justified on social policy grounds, has increasingly been promoted on grounds of crime prevention. According to the works of criminologists such as Wilson and Kelling (1982), crime generates the gradual erosion of neighbourhoods and community integration. According to their 'broken windows' thesis, anti-social behaviour, or 'incivilities', such as vandalism, have the effect of rending the fabric of community apart and accelerating a downward spiral of community degeneration. It is the cycle of crime rather than the cycle of deprivation which is now the significant issue in urban social problems. Instead of social workers and community activists 'mobilising' the poor and disadvantaged, the forces of law and order are invited to step in and fill the 'vacuum' left by the lack of appropriate social authority: the police become the guardians of a collapsing moral order.

Broken windows

In the 1960s there was an optimism in academic and official circles about the capacities of neighbourhoods and communities to work together and raise the profile of their area; the growth of concern about crime since then has coincided with an emerging scepticism, and pessimism, about the capacity of these neighbourhoods in the 'inner city' to change effectively either their own values or the environment they inhabit. This latter assumption has left its impact on the ways in which crime prevention strategies have been devised and structured. Official scepticism about the ability, or willingness, of 'problem' estates and run-down inner-city areas to 'pull themselves up by their own bootstraps' (Loney, 1981) reinforced an emerging consensus that simply pumping public money into these localities was wasteful and pointless. Instead, resources should be reserved for those city zones in danger of 'tipping' downwards into this state of social disintegration. The Wilson and Kelling strategy demanded state intervention when the first window was broken; once the downward spiral of neglect, vandalism and despair was under way, it became difficult, even impossible, to arrest the decline. The logic of this argument has led to several interlocking strategies: firstly, intervention in those communities where there is a danger of decline, as outlined above; secondly, protection for those respectable areas in close proximity to dangerous localities, in the form of neighbourhood watch and similar crime prevention measures, which throw a kind of *cordon sanitaire* around them. In this way the contemporary concern about crime and community has expanded from a belief that crime originates within communities to an insistence that communities need to be protected from an invasion (Hope and Shaw, 1988) from without. The notion of 'invasion' by an 'outside threat' is an important one because it sums up some crucial aspects of recent crime debates. The concern that communities are prey to criminal behaviour is complemented on an individual level by the image of the isolated, vulnerable 'victim', but also on a broader level by the image of the national community itself under attack from an array of alien forces. The debate about crime and community has not simply shifted from an emphasis on crime originating within the community to an emphasis on the external threat, as Hope and Shaw and others have suggested; rather the debate has 'polarised' and now separates communities, with some localities displaying a tendency to generate crime and others being the target of crime. We shall discuss the features of these criminal communities below.

We wish to point out here that this increasing emphasis on crime prevention has complemented shifts that have taken place in social work practice itself. The 'nothing works' ideology that became embedded in social work practice in the wake of the 'post-treatment epoch', has meant that many social workers have had to accept the underlying principles of the crime prevention movement. For, if 'nothing works' in face-to-face work with client groups, if crime is an opportunistic, haphazard and random process, if treatment is a non-starter, then why not become involved in local crime prevention initiatives which attempt to keep out crime rather than be seen to perpetuate discredited treatment models which only serve to enlarge and label client groups? Moreover, taking a 'realist' stance in relation to crime challenges those common assumptions that social workers do not take crime seriously, or are only interested in protecting the interests of delinquents and deviants. Becoming involved in local crime prevention panels, as many probation officers and intermediate treatment workers have done, promotes good inter-agency cooperation and enhances their reputation while, apparently, doing little harm: a safe and even potentially fruitful option. We shall have a good deal to say below both about the impact of crime prevention, harmless and otherwise, and about multi-agency work. Firstly, though, we shall pursue some of the themes about involvement in communities and community involvement in crime prevention a little further. Let us summarise the major points we have made thus far: firstly, we have suggested that there has been a marked shift in emphasis in official thinking about the problem of problem communities, which can be summarised as a shift from an emphasis on their disadvantages towards a stress on their dangerousness; it follows from this that, secondly, the danger is perceived in terms of the threat these communities pose to society, either because these communities contaminate adjoining neighbourhoods or because they target the more affluent areas of the city for their crimes.

The law-and-order society

It needs emphasising that this process has been influenced by wider shifts in political and official thinking and has not emerged in a political vacuum. Stuart Hall prophesied in 1980 that we were 'Drifting into a Law and Order Society', a society more 'disciplinary' and 'authoritarian' (Hall, 1980). This drift, to which he referred as a 'deep and decisive movement', is characterised by an obsession with issues of crime and law and order. They have become what Antonio Gramsci called 'the morbid symptoms' of our particular social crisis (Gramsci, 1971). A number of writers influenced by what has become known as the 'Neo-Gramscian' analysis of contemporary societies have followed Stuart Hall in identifying the links between the increasing concern with law, order and crime, and an emerging authoritarianism in British politics. Terms such as 'authoritarian populism', 'social authoritarianism', 'the authoritarian state', draw

our attention to a move in consensual politics toward a more coercive, stronger form of government, determined to reverse the decline
in British society by reinstating traditional beliefs and values. What
has been called 'neo-conservatism' or the 'New Right' has combined
a fierce advocacy of the free market with a commitment to firm
government in the law-and-order field. What distinguishes the analysis of Hall and others is their concern to show the inter-relatedness of
economic, cultural and political concerns in the New Right philosophy: the way each has become woven into an overall picture of
'Britain in crisis'. Sim, Scraton and Gordon summarise the major
themes of the new right thus:

> They drew together several folk devils which became plausible explana-
> tions for the economic and social 'decline' of Great Britain: the power of
> the unions; the rise of the scrounger; the escalation of crime; the threat of
> terrorism; the decline of moral values; the subversion of democracy. Each
> of these carefully constructed images, emphasised and reinforced by a
> right wing media eager to cultivate and mobilise prejudices against any
> progressive developments around race, gender, class, unemployment and
> poverty became synonymous with the 'breakdown' of British society. The
> demand was for a return to an old order – one based upon the pillars of
> 'morality' and 'discipline' – the claimed values of Victorian Britain (Sim *et
> al*, 1987, p 60)

We do not intend to dwell on the various dimensions of this overall
picture. Rather, we wish to draw attention to the fact that debates
about crime and community need to be placed in the wider context of
social and political change: these have left their mark on the ways in
which crime has become identified as a central issue in contemporary
politics. Crime problems have become a vivid 'metaphor' for a host
of evils which have beset this country. Also the notion of 'community' itself has played a role in determining the direction of crime prevention strategies; as we have already intimated, there are communities and communities, some of which require protection whereas
others require policing. The problem is that the notion of community
has not escaped unscathed in the political struggles in Britain. Our
argument is that the image of community has been recruited by the
Conservative drift in British politics. Britain's communities, along
with its culture, democratic processes, legal institutions, etc, are considered to be a unique national achievement, an achievement which
is constantly imperilled by a variety of dangerous forces. Modern
Conservatism, despite its radicalism in economic spheres, is profoundly nostalgic for an imaginary Albion of settled communities,
built upon ties of kith and kinship. This nostalgia for a 'national past'
(Wright, 1985) invades the present attitude towards those whose
sense of belonging seems 'more makeshift and improvised' (Wright,
1985, p 234) than ours, and whose cultural roots are in national communities different from our own. 'Community' is not, therefore, a

neutral term describing any collective of people, rather it has been used strategically to separate groups in our society, each with a varying degree of commitment to the British way of life. The link between 'nation' and 'community' is an important one. In his study of the rise of nationalism Benedict Anderson has described the nation precisely as an 'Imagined Community', a community conceived of as possessing a 'deep, horizontal comradeship' (Anderson, 1983, p 16), irrespective of any real inequalities within it. Anderson suggests that nations can be distinguished by the particular 'style with which they are imagined' (p 15). It could be argued that that style of recent British nationalism, certainly as it has been promoted by the Conservative right, has been to imagine itself as beleaguered and undermined, its sense of community evaporating and its unique national achievements threatened by alien forces.

The racialisation of crime

This sense of threat, the fears about crime, the concerns about community, which figure in contemporary political debate and have aided the swing to the right in Britain, have been decisively marked by concerns about race. One may suggest, for example, that the debate about communities has been transformed by the emergence of race as a dominant concern. Here, debate has focused upon a presumed absence of 'community' within racial minority groups; or at least the presence of a kind of community different in form and content from 'ours'. The philosophy of the community action approach rested upon implicit assumptions that there was a core of shared values within society, around which agreement could be reached and change achieved. The emergence of what Barker (1981) has called the 'New Racism', linked to the New Right generally, has explicitly challenged these assumptions by promoting a view of nationhood and 'Britishness' which asserts the fundamental uniqueness of national cultures. The New Racism suggests that attempts to integrate communities are misguided and dangerous; they can only result in tension, conflict and violence: those infamous 'rivers of blood'.

It is worth exploring the issue of race in the context of crime and community at some length because of the central role 'race' has played in formulating the agenda for debate about crime and community. The work of Barker in defining the phenomenon of the New Racism has complemented an emerging critique of British racism originating in the works of the Birmingham Centre for Contemporary Cultural Studies under Stuart Hall, and developed further by John Solomos, Paul Gilroy and others. Works such as *Policing the Crisis*, *The Empire Strikes Back* and more recently Paul Gilroy's *There Ain't No Black in the Union Jack* provide a valuable starting point because of the way they link the 'crisis' in British society to issues wider than the straightforward economic ones. The British crisis has been a crisis of the 'British way of life', under threat from a host of enemies; in particular, from an 'alien wedge' of immigrants who do not share 'our' culture and way of life. The centrality of race to the particular way in which the crisis has been explained to people is crucial to this analysis: firstly, because it has become a way in which the responsibilty for 'our' decline as a once great nation can be transferred onto an alien force; secondly, because the New Racism appeals to the nation, to the 'imagined community', rather than to sectarian interests based upon class, and has been successful in uniting a wide diversity of otherwise conflicting interests – the political left as well as the right. The latter has been possible, Paul Gilroy asserts, because the New Racism does not focus primarily on colour difference as the basis for its attack, but plays, rather, upon cultural difference as a means of making 'our national crisis intelligible' (Gilroy, 1987). He goes on:

> . . . its novelty lies in the capacity to link discourses of patriotism, nationalism, xenophobia, Englishness, Britishness, militarism, and gender differences into a complex system which gives 'race' its contemporary meaning. These themes combine to provide a new definition of 'race' in terms of culture and identity' (p 43).

The New Racism constructs a unity based upon a shared national identity from which black people are excluded.

Not all foreign cultures are viewed in the same way within the New Racism. People of Afro-Caribbean descent are regarded as having no coherent cultural identity, whereas those from the Asian subcontinent are considered to possess a coherence – albeit one based upon principles radically different from our own. This is an important distinction and has implications for the ways in which these communities are viewed and responded to by powerful agencies in contemporary Britain. While communities of Afro-Caribbean descent are considered a problem because their cultures are disorganised and fragmented, Asian communities are considered a problem because they are over-organised and difficult to penetrate. In both cases an implicit comparison is being made between these alien cultures and some supposedly coherent and identifiable 'Britishness', shared by the majority of the population. The issues of crime and law and order are an important feature of the way in which the New Racism constructs culture as the primary arena of conflict and tension. 'Respect for the law' is represented as a key characteristic of 'Britishness': 'their' incapacity to understand the law, or their willingness to flout its authority openly represents a crucial difference between our cultures. The New Racism elevates the rule of law to the status of a 'unique and important cultural achievement' (Gilroy, 1987, p 74), understood and appreciated only by those who share the common national characteristics and values which have brought it into being. The importance of race in the overall 'swing to the right' in British politics is given prominence in the works of Gilroy and others. In their thoughtful study of the 'mugging' incidents in Handsworth in Birmingham in the early 1970s, Hall *et al* (1978) draw our attention to the ways in which crime can become 'racialised' and become a potent symbol of our national decline. In their view the 'moral panics' about mugging were influential in constructing an 'authoritarian consensus' (Hall *et al*, 1978, p 339) in Britain which increasingly saw the solution to Britain's crisis in terms of a return to law and order and the 'repatriation' of alien cultures to their places of origin.

The notion of mugging as a form of crime cannot in their opinion be understood outside an emerging perception of black people generally, and black youth in particular, as more criminally inclined than the white community: mugging has become synonymous with black crime Bridges, 1983). In this way black communities become 'criminalised' and their culture is portrayed as essentially deviant, fragmented and incapable of instilling the correct values into its young people. The circuit is completed with this shift from community and culture to the pathological family systems which underpin them. New Right philosophy gives the family an almost sacred status within social life. Unlike institutions in the public domain, which are artificial and transient, the family is conceived as natural and permanent, above history and politics, rooted in biology rather than society (Levitas, 1986).

Of course such an analysis ignores the extent to which families differ enormously over time and are themselves conditioned by shifts in economic and political structures, and the extent to which the state and social policies have themselves shaped and fashioned the modern family (Donzelot, 1980: Ennew, 1986). The nuclear family is presented to us as a natural, instinctive organism rather than as an historically specific institution, formed by a range of social forces. It is then used as a yardstick by which other forms of family life are measured as 'normal' or 'deviant'. Alien communities are distinguishable by their incapacity, or unwillingness, to adapt to the pattern of family life considered normal in the host society. The fact that this so-called 'norm' is far from being the norm amongst white Britons matters little. What matters is the image that the vision of the British family conjures up: an image of a settled, harmonious, wholesome and orderly unit, instilling the correct social values into its children, and capable of prudent housekeeping without needing the interference of the state and its army of functionaries to prop it up. Those Victorian values, so admired by Mrs Thatcher, are unmistakably the values of the Victorian family – or rather those 'imagined' values, which may bear only a passing resemblance to the real thing.

Britain is not the only western society obsessed with the sacred relics of its history. New Right philosophy in the United States has a similar preoccupation with an imagined past, although, following Anderson's assertion that nations are distinguishable by the 'style' in which they imagine themselves as communities, the American version of the past has its own unique characteristics – a Hollywood-style production featuring the independent pioneer and his kin, braving the wilderness and taming a continent. If Mrs Thatcher's version of an ideal family looks something like 'Upstairs Downstairs' then Ronald Reagan's is surely 'The Little House on the Prairie'! Flippancy aside, the imagined past again includes an imagined family as a core ingredient, something which gives permanence and continuity to the nation's progress through time. This ideal family, like the communities it supports and nurtures, becomes another yardstick against which other families and communities can be measured and, frequently, found wanting.

The black family has been at the centre of concern in a variety of ways and on a variety of themes, stretching from educational issues through to the more recent concern with crime. What tends to unite these assorted 'debates' about the black family is an overall concern with its presumed incapacity to provide an effective means of socialising its children, due to such factors as heredity, culture and marital instability. In the 1960s in the USA prominent liberals such as Daniel Moynihan (soon, like other disenchanted liberals, such as Nathan Glazer and Norman Podhoretz, to become a prominent supporter of the New Right) were arguing that the fragmentation of the 'negro family' lay behind the problem of the black community as a whole. Moynihan asserted that unstable marriages and the 'crumbling' black family led to the high proportion of households headed by women in black communities, which proved unviable as a source of stable child-rearing (Moynihan, 1965). The disorganised family was the root-cause of the perpetual cycle of poverty in black communities. This stress upon fragmentation and disorder as a dynamic cultural process has been criticised for its tendency to 'victim blame', that is to lay the responsibility for poverty and deprivation onto the black community and other poor people, rather than on structural factors in society. The tendency has found its way into British theory and practice in fields such as education and social work. In the latter field Paul Stubbs (1988a) and Lena Dominelli (1988) have pointed to a dominant tradition in social work of perceiving black families as essentially pathological, inadequate and unstable.

Many of these assumptions about the black family have resurfaced in the debate about black criminality – not surprisingly since they provide a ready-made set of 'explanations' for the phenomenon.

Black youths are more predisposed to crime because of the lack of authority and control within their disorderly, makeshift familes. Crime, particularly 'street crime', becomes the 'front line' between two cultural worlds. Nowhere are the links between policing and safeguarding the values of British society in the face of this alien onslaught made more explicit than in this statement of Sir Kenneth Newman, the then Commissioner of the Metropolitan Police, in 1983. Here he captures the spirit of Wilson and Kelling's invitation for policing to become a moral enterprise:

> Throughout London there are locations where unemployed youth – often black youths – congregate; where the sale and purchase of drugs, the exchange of stolen property and illegal drinking and gaming is not uncommon. The youths regard these locations as their territory. Police are viewed as intruders, the symbol of authority – largely white authority – in a society that is responsible for all their grievances about unemployment, prejudice and discrimination. . . . If allowed to continue, locations with these characteristics assume symbolic importance and negative symbolism of the inability of the police to maintain order. Their existence encourages law breaking elsewhere, affects public perceptions of police effectiveness, heightens fear of crime and reniforces a phenomenon of urban decay (cited in Gilroy and Sim, 1985, p 100).

The claim that street crime is a feature of the specific cultures of black people has influenced observers who would place themslves on the left of the political spectrum, as well as those of the right. The 'new realist' criminology has been critical of what its adherents consider to be the tendency for radical criminology to underestimate the extent to which crime damages ordinary working-class people; criminals, they argue, should not be romanticised as Robin Hood characters re-expropriating the wealth stolen from the poor by the rich, nor should their criminal behaviour be justified as a primitive sort of class politics. Working-class communities are usually the victims of working-class crime, and these communities deserve protection from those who prey upon them. This dimension of their argument may be relatively uncontentious; however, their desire to 'take crime seriously' has led to criticism of their position, on the grounds that they accept too readily the idea that certain cultures spontaneously generate crime. They argue that black people in Britain have become 'marginalised' in urban society due to their powerlessness and discrimination by white society; this has led to the creation of a 'culture of discontent' and 'despair' as black youths strive to find an identity in a hostile environment (Lea and Young, 1982). They go on to assert that this culture manifests itself in higher crime rates amongst blacks than amongst whites. In a passage that has come in for strong criticism, they argue:

> Cultures which grow out of adversity and oppression are as likely to be

predatory as progressive. Crime abounds in such communities and whereas much of it has no significance (i.e. cannabis smoking), other elements such as street robbery and interpersonal violence are seriously anti-social (Lea and Young, 1982, p 10).

This attempt to link a supposedly higher rate of crime amongst blacks to the presence of a particular culture of frustrated aspirations amongst black youth in particular has been criticised by many observers. It has been argued that this analysis merely apes the pronouncements of right-wing racists, eager to display black cultures as essentially criminogenic and therefore a threat to social order (Scraton, 1987); that the analysis rests upon questionable statistics on 'mugging' rates which, it is suggested, have been concocted by the police in order to justify the heavy policing of black areas of London; and the importance of culture as an explanation for crime is over-valued at the expense of factors such as poverty (Gilroy, 1987).

The emphasis on culture, therefore, in debates about law and order and crime can easily lead to situations in which whole communities are identified as criminally inclined: especially so since this discussion of community has been influenced by an established practice of viewing black families as pathological. As we have already suggested, the very notion of community itself is not a neutral term, but has been invested with a particular set of meanings; in contemporary society the term has symbolised the loss of traditional solidarity, authority and 'rootedness' (Levitas, 1986) based upon a set of shared values (respect for the law being an important one) which have been eroded by the impersonality and complexity of modern urban society, and contaminated by the influx of alien cultures with different value systems. These factors have influenced the way debates about crime have been conducted in recent years. These, however, have not been the only concerns. It is tempting to conclude that the whole upsurge of interest in crime has been manipulated and controlled by the New Right and its allies within the state; that the Conservative right somehow 'owns' the crime debate. This has certainly been a consistent argument of ultra-pessimists such as Scraton. We should like to suggest that the debate is rather more complex, and that issues have arisen within it that have actually created problems for the New Right thinking and for the management of crime by the state. Opening the crime debate has been like opening a Pandora's Box, and its contents have included a few surprises.

Re-focusing the crime debate

We have argued that the drift into the law-and-order society has been encouraged by an increased concern about the effects of crime on the social fabric of society. The strength of the Conservative argument for more policing and a tougher stand on crime is based upon the extent to which crime has become a metaphor for a wide variety of contemporary anxieties; this has been a soruce of strength for the New Right, but conversely, it may also be a source of weakness. So much has been invested in the crime issue that it has spilled over into a range of issues far beyond the scope of those simple concerns over mugging and similar forms of moral panic which are easily manipulated by the popular press. In his classic text *Folk Devils and Moral Panics* (1973), Stan Cohen correctly identified the role of the folk devil as a hate figure on whom popular anxieties could be safely vented. The 'mugger' was the most recent addition to the gallery of popular folk devils and represented dominant concerns at the time about street crime, urban disorder and race. We should like to suggest that current images of the crime problem, while they in no way remove the tendency to racialise certain types of crime, are too complex and diffuse to be contained within a single, unified hate symbol: the skinhead or the black mugger, for example. The debate about crime has broadened in several important respects; it has become a debate about how crime is managed; why particular types of crime are given priority and others are not; about the real needs and demands of victims; about the effectiveness of policing; about 'hidden' forms of crime; and about the prejudices and practices of the judiciary and the police. The weakness of the new Conservatism lies, therefore, in the fact that 'taking crime seriously' can draw attention not only to forms of crime beyond the New Right agenda, but can include criticism of crime control agencies themselves.

One of the distinguishing features of the new Conservatism has been its mix of traditional authoritarianism and populism. This has proved successful in promoting the image of the Conservatives as the 'party of law and order': the only political grouping that reflects popular anxiety about crime. In the 1970s the Conservative right could safely argue that they alone 'spoke for victims of crime' when they called for a return to stronger policing and stiffer sentencing in courts. Research has revealed the public generally, including even victims of crime themselves, to be less punitive and vengeful than this simple image would suggest (Hough and Moxon, 1985); victims of crime and the radical right do not necessarily speak with one harmonious voice, and what victims really want may differ in many respects from what the New Right wants for them (see Chapter 7).

The image of the victim of crime was used in a crusade to strengthen the authoritarian apparatuses of the state. Those who have been active in formulating new initiatives designed to improve services to victims have suggested that the authoritarian and disciplinary arms of the state, while they may use victims to justify punitive sentencing, are not deeply concerned with involving victims in the judicial process itself. Indeed, the process may render them even more powerless, or become itself a source of stress and anxiety. Resolving some of the real problems of being a victim may, in fact, involve a loosening of the control of the state and allowing the victims to define for themselves what they consider to be a resolution of their problem. Loosening the bonds of state control, on the other hand, threatens to undermine the authoritarian thrust of the New Right. Many who so vociferously spoke for the needs of the victim now speak with equal force for the need to maintain the authority and power of the state: hence Enoch Powell, the champion of little old ladies and other victims of black crime in the 1960s and 1970s, has now become the staunchest defender of the full majesty of the law in all its abstract omnipotence, when he criticises the idea that victims and offenders may wish to resolve their problems via mediation rather than through the criminal justice system (Powell, 1985). Clearly, it is one thing to speak for victims but quite another to allow them to speak for themselves.

It is a reflection of the complexity of criminal justice issues that a process which began in the 1970s by highlighting victims' demands for punishment and implicitly condemning the welfare services for not paying enough attention to the interests of victims (being too pre-occupied with the 'needs' of offenders), has become, in the 1980s, increasingly concerned with the inadequacy of the punishment machine itself as a vehicle for meeting victims' needs. Where there have been improvements in the services for victims they have tended to come about on the periphery of the system, or outside it alto-gether. They have been achieved through new initiatives by agencies at the executive level (some multi-agency reparation and mediation schemes, for example); through the use of the voluntary sector as a supplement to the established system (victim support services of various kinds); or through self-help organisations such as rape-crisis centres, women's refuges, and so on. Moreover, such initiatives have firmly placed the welfare issue back on the agenda. Victims of crime may, indeed, be angry and seek revenge, but they may also have a range of feelings and anxieties, left behind in the wake of the event, which cannot be resolved simply by prosecuting the offender (see Chapter 7). Victims may also discover that the punishment machine exists to process offenders rather than to help the victims.

The interest in the victims of crime has provided a further source of discomfort for the New Right theories of social life. Those, like Powell, who so strongly support the letter of the law on certain issues, may be the first to resist the intervention of the law in other domains – for example, when legal intervention threatens the privacy of the family. Indeed, they may support instead those very 'informal' mechanisms for 'resolving' problems which they so vehemently oppose otherwise. Increasingly the debate about victims of crime has been widened to include forms of crime that challenge many features of the new Conservatism, particularly its belief in the sacred unity of the family. The police and the legal system have come under intense pressure in recent years to take seriously forms of crime that were once considered not to be real crimes at all. Along with a growing demand to 'deinstitutionalise' the resolution of certain types of criminal acts, there has been a demand to criminalise fully other forms, such as 'domestic' violence, racially motivated attacks and sexual abuse of children. For while certain types of crime are what we might call 'over-policed', others may be 'under-policed'.

Policing violence against women and children

Violence against women and children in the public domain, through a sudden assault by a stranger, could be made to fit neatly into the established discourse on crime. In contrast to this established view, however, there has been an increasing emphasis in recent years on the problems women and children face within the private domain of the family itself. This has led to a critical examination of the ways these crimes are dealt with by the police and the courts, and their tendency tacitly to decriminalise such crimes has come under criticism. Feminist theorists have successfully placed these issues onto the official and public agenda and highlighted the 'normality' of abuse of and violence against women and children as the mundane features of a society built upon patriarchal power (Kelly, 1988: Kelly and Radford, 1987). Highlighting such problems brings the debate about crime into the very heartland of contemporary Conservatism and threatens to undermine some of its core assumptions about social life.

In the New Right philosophy the family occupies a unique position as a natural order, an authentic and permanent body counterposed to the artificial and transient institutions of the wider society. This assertion complements a traditional set of patriarchal values which also normalises the subjugation of women and children as a biologically rooted necessity. Within this perspective certain forms of violence against women and children can be sanctioned in various ways. For instance, it is the duty of women to satisfy the sexual demands of their husbands, and therefore 'rape' cannot exist within the family. If a woman does not provide these services then she is responsible for the consequences, due to the fact that men are sexually incontinent and driven by the impulses to penetrate and procreate; they cannot then be held totally to blame if they forcibly take what nature has ordained as their right, or at least seek alternatives. This belief has real consequences for the victims of sexual and other forms of violence within the family. In a court case in February 1989 a judge gave a suspended prison sentence to a man who raped his 12-year-old

stepdaughter, justifying his leniency on the grounds that the offender's wife was not satisfying his sexual needs (*The Guardian*, 26
February 1989).

This belief is not confined to the conservative wing of the judiciary. Social work has also been criticised for accepting models of
family dynamics which hold mothers responsible for the sexual abuse
of children when they are not fulfilling their role as sexual providers
(Nelson, 1986; Hooper, 1988; Saraga and Macleod, 1988). In the
area of sexual abuse of children there are many more taboos, and few
would attempt to justify it; there are, however, a range of standard
'explanations' as to why it occurs which help to 'get men off the
hook' (Hooper, 1988). Other forms of abuse of children (physical
abuse, acts of mental cruelty, emotional neglect, and so on) are to
some extent sanctioned and made acceptable by the standards of traditional family life; indeed strict discipline and control are considered to be virtues in themselves, part of that deeply mourned moral
order of Victorian Britain. Of course extreme forms of physical abuse
and neglect are outlawed in contemporary society, but other forms
are, many observers argue, normal in most families: the psychoana-
lyst Alice Miller suggests that 'tormenting one's children is a legiti-
mate part of child rearing' (Miller, 1985, p 79). In a similar vein, the
anthropologist Judith Ennew asserts that:

> In many societies, including our own, adult power over children is so
> absolute that in a sense all children are abused and all adults are abusers
> (Ennew, 1986, p 141).

The question of the abuse of children has surfaced in a dramatic manner with the Cleveland crisis; we do not intend to dwell on it here as
the issues have been well rehearsed elsewhere (Campbell, 1988). The
crisis in Cleveland has, irrespective of the rights and wrongs of the
particular case, placed the issue of sexual violence toward children
firmly on the agenda of social work and other agencies and has intensified demands for more multi-agency work (see below). What is
interesting in the specific context of New Right philosophy about the
family is the potential the issue contains for opening up this private
realm to scrutiny. Blagg and Stubbs argue that the issue is potentially
very 'subversive':

> By actually encouraging children to speak about what goes on in the
> family, one is rendering public that which tends to remain most private
> and secret in our society. The principle of the 'family' as a sacred unity, at
> least in its white, nuclear guise, goes deep into our cultural psyche, so that
> any attack upon it is tantamount to undermining society itself. Attacks
> have to be repulsed by all means possible, including the use of images ren-
> dering the attacks alien and foreign to our 'civilised' way of life. Responses
> to the apparent discovery of large-scale sexual abuse in Cleveland, making
> references to 'Salem' conjuring up images of witchcraft and inappropriate

female power, and to 'Stalin's Russia', where children were encouraged to denounce their parents to the state, are two obvious examples of this process (Blagg and Stubbs, 1988, p 14)

The fact that sexual abuse is assumed to take place in all types of family, irrespective of social class, adds a further subversive dimenson to the issue, because it weakens another basic tenet of established orthodoxy in the debates about families, the belief that sexual and other forms of violence are produced in certain disorganised, dysfunctional and pathological family systems. The dominance of the family dysfunction model of sexual violence has been further eroded by a growing body of work claiming that the problem lies in the nature of male sexuality generally rather than in specific deviant family structures (Glaser and Frosh, 1988; Kelly, 1988).

We are suggesting, therefore that the debate about crime has become fragmented and, to some extent, separated from the preoccupation with crime on the street as the major area of concern. Pressure from women's groups and feminists has provided the major impetus for change. Of course, anxieties about street crime still exert a powerful influence on thinking about crime. However, the issue of sexual violence against women and children, as it has been presented by feminists, has modified the debate in several important respects: firstly, attacks by strangers in the public realm have been set in a broader context of the danger women and children face in other domains, notably in the family; secondly, women and children are in danger, on the street and in the home, from 'men' as a group generally rather than some marginal folk devil, such as the black mugger. Moreover, the issue has concentrated attention upon the way in which women in particular are treated by state agencies and the judiciary when victimised by male violence.

In the United States pressure from women's groups has led to a number of steps designed to improve services for victims of rape and domestic violence. There the issue of official responses to sexual violence in the home has been more forcefully debated than in this country, and a number of initiatives have been introduced intended to improve services for women. Legislative changes, such as the 1984 Family Violence Prevention and Services Act, which encouraged the development of programmes aimed at preventing family violence and provided funds for individual states to initiate services for victims of violence, reflect an increasing awareness of the necessity for the authorities to take seriously crimes of this kind. One experiment in Minneapolis, begun in 1984, attempted to reduce the incidence of repeated violence against women in the home by encouraging the police to make arrests of male offenders rather than 'resolving' the matter informally via mediation between the parties or by encouraging separation. After six months it was found that arrest was twice as likely to deter the offender as mediation or separating the parties (Cohen, 1987). Other experiments conducted in the USA and in Canada reveal that firm intervention in domestic violence which effectively criminalises the abuse can be effective in protecting women and children from subsequent violence (Nuttall, 1988). One interesting spin-off of the increased attention given to the issue in the USA has been an increase in the numbers of women who now actively sue the police for failing to arrest, or for making false arrests, following domestic violence cases: in one case a woman successfully sued a local police department for not protecting her and her son from a violent husband and was awarded $12.6 million (Cohen, 1987). Of course many aspects of the American approach are particular to its own judicial system and would be difficult to reproduce in Britain. In this country we lack a system of constitutional rights which could be used to establish judicial protection for women and children in a similar way.

Agencies in this country have been appreciably slower to recognise the problems faced by women and children who are victims of violence within the family. Dobash and Dobash's study (1979) illustrated that such violence was not a feature of isolated, deviant family structures, but was an established means whereby men control women and children within the family. Moreover the authors identified a tendency on the part of the authorities to minimise the seriousness of violence within the home. Blagg *et al* (1988) noted that the very term 'domestic' was used to denote an incident that was not a 'real' crime and did not require serious investigation by the police; other research on the occupational culture of the police has demonstrated that 'domestics' are conceived as 'rubbish' work (Smith and Gray, 1983), and noted a reluctance on the part of the police to prosecute in such cases (Faragher, 1985; Pahl, 1985). This practice of downgrading the seriousness of violence within the home is not confined to the police but extends to social workers as well (Maynard, 1985; Borkowski *et al*, 1983). This suggests that such indifference may be a product of deeply rooted patriarchal attitudes rather than of particular professional cultures. There are signs, on the other hand, that agencies are becoming more responsive to the needs of victims of rape and family violence. Recent concern over the treatment women receive following rape incidents has led to a number of changes in agency practice. The Metropolitan Police have introduced special suites, staffed by women police officers, in liaison with the social services, in order to reduce the trauma for victims; similarly, the use of women doctors to carry out sensitive examinations on rape victims, and children who have been sexually abused, is also being widely encouraged (Kilker, 1988). The policing of domestic violence still raises particular difficulties: change in police practice in this area has to overcome the problems posed by the attitudes of ordinary police officers who are called to deal with such incidents, and these may prove more difficult to change.

Responses to racism

The response of state authorities to racial attacks against black people has also come under scrutiny in recent years. We have already discussed the ways in which black communities have been criminalised and are popularly seen as playing a crucial part in the alarmingly rising rates of crime. In the light of this it is hardly surprising that black people find it difficult to enlist official support against racism, even when this takes a violent form. Indeed, so deeply have images of black criminality penetrated debates about crime that black people may find it impossible to be considered 'victims' of any crime at all (Pearson *et al* (1989), and may be treated as 'offenders' when coming forward to report incidents in which they had been victims. We shall take up the issue of discrimination against black people in the criminal justice system in Chapter 4; here we shall briefly consider the problems of policing racism in contemporary Britain. We have already suggested that state agencies perpetuate racism in their practice. With Peason *et al* (1989), we would argue that the police, by virtue of the power they wield in society, perpetuate racist attitudes in a particularly active manner. Studies such as that carried out by Smith and Gray (1983) starkly reveal a profound degree of racism within the Metropolitan Police, with racist jokes and language a common currency within the police's 'canteen culture'.

The problem is more than just one of racist attitudes. It is also a problem of racist practices: Pearson *et al* (1983) argue that racism operates on a number of levels and takes a number of different forms. These go beyond simple racist attitudes to influence the ways in which even well-intentioned reforms in the race area operate, in the sense that they fail to take into consideration adequately, or discount, the feelings and experiences of black people, in much the same way that the distress and suffering of women are frequently minimised by placing a 'domestic' label on crimes within the home. Pearson and his colleagues note several areas of concern in the relationship between the police and the racial minorities. Firstly, they note a tendency to 'over-police' black communities, when certain types of street crime or public order offences are given priority (through intensive use of powers to stop and search, for example). Secondly, there is a tendency to 'under-police' crimes against black people such as racial attacks. Thirdly, there is the issue of the way in which the police respond to black people, and the problems they have in policing their own racism. The police, then, find it difficult to see black people as victims; they are usually considered to be potential or actual offenders. Hence people from an Asian background who report racial attacks are asked first to show their passports, and a check is made on their immigration status. Finally, attempts to build links with communities via a 'community relations' approach can actually intensify discrimination against black residents on estates when this approach is made through already existing bodies such as tenants' associations which tend to be predominantly white organisations (Pearson *et al*, 1989).

This tendency reinforces a point we made earlier. Communities are not unified entities but are made up of a range of different and frequently unequal and antagonistic groups; neighbourhood associations may represent the interests of one particular section within a locality rather than the community as a whole. When agencies, not only the police, consult the community they often speak to 'representatives' who may represent only one of these interest groups. Sampson *et al* (1988) observe a similar tendency for the police to respond to the demands of powerful white interest groups in their study of police–community relations on 'Gabriel's Walk' in London. In this case the police responded to the demand of more recently arrived white middle-class residents who believed that drug use was lowering the tone of the neighbourhood (the black community was split between those who considered the soft drugs sold locally to be relatively harmless and those who frowned on all drug use). A gradual and cautious programme designed to reduce drug use in the area in consultation with the community was set aside in favour of a new policy of saturation policing. The authors note the consequences:

> As a result, amidst levels of policing which had to be seen to be believed, the fragile consensus broke down abruptly. Moreover, a further consequence was the criminalisation of *all* black people within the vicinity as potential suspects for 'stop and search' operations. This did no good, either for the quality of life of many residents of Gabriel's Walk, or for police–community relations in the area. Indeed, it offers some of the most vivid evidence for the way in which 'multi-agency' and 'community-orientated' strategies can actually *increase* pre-existing tensions within a neighbourhood by giving preferential treatment to some sectional interests within the locality and not to others (Sampson *et al*, 1988, 486/487).

The tendency to give preferential treatment to white residents in these situations further reinforces the feeling amongst black groups that consultation is a waste of time, and they may choose not to be represented at all on locally based consultation committees. Clearly the police were willing to respond in a heavy-handed way to the drug problem on Gabriel's Walk, because the issue fitted into their already constructed images of black communities as drug-infested, with a consequent need to police such a 'symbolic location' heavily. Once this was set in motion, other images of black criminality as expressive of a general criminal culture amongst black people legitimated a policy of 'stop and search' which treated all black people as *a priori* suspects. Here again we see how the practical job of policing is informed by wider cultural images of certain communities as being a fundamental problem in our society. Even though the black community on Gabriel's Walk was more settled than the new middle-class groups, their interests were subordinated to the demands of the white newcomers.

This tendency is repeated in other situations where black people are considered to have less of a claim to belong to a particular area than white people, even when the latter are new arrivals. This can only be understood in the context of admittance to the 'imagined community' as outlined earlier; admittance to this can have a class as well as a racial tag attached to it. Patrick Wright illustrates this process in Stoke Newington which, like Gabriel's Walk, was becoming gentrified and redeveloped. The newcomers to the area could lay claim to the historic ancestry of the area; they came to unearth and cherish its imperilled relics of the past. The local overgrown grave-yard becomes a setting for a 'gothic stroll', whereas the local working-class people think it is a health hazard (Wright, 1985, p 236). Being in a place, therefore, is not the same thing as 'belonging' to it. Some can lay greater claim to represent the area because of cultural continuities with our imagined past. There are parallels here with the New Racism; although black people may have legal status as British subjects, they can never truly belong to the imagined community of the nation because they do not share the same cultural values (cf Gilroy, 1987), or the same 'deep horizontal comradeship'.

Working together

We are suggesting here that the crime issue has broadened significantly since the 1970s, which were characterised by the unchallenged ascendancy of a virulent New Right critique of social democracy and its incapacity to resolve the many crises of British society. The mugger, the scrounger and other folk devils were children of the permissive society, undermined by an interventionist state which sapped the moral fibre of communities and families. The lack of an adequate challenge to this world-view in the crime and law-and-order field was not remedied by a left criminology self-consciously disdainful of muddying its hands with practical issues of law and order, preferring instead to await the imminent and inevitable collapse of capitalism. At this time the beleaguered apparatuses of social democracy had few defenders and many critics, although many on the left began to rally to the support of the welfare state when it was strategically too late to save many of its most cherished principles. Social work has had even fewer defenders than other areas of state welfare. The Conservative backlash in the 1970s was able to exploit a general feeling that social work was either failing to fulfil its role within society or was intervening in ways which were detrimental to the self-esteem of the individuals and families who came within its domain. For the right wing, social work incarnated the very worst features of social democracy because it undermined family responsibility; for the left it was part of a state conspiracy to control and depoliticise the working class who became 'trapped within welfare' (Simpkin, 1979). Social work has been placed in a 'Catch 22' situation by the policy shifts of recent years. It has had to acccede to pressures to shed many of its more liberal, client-centred approaches to its task and take on a more policing and controlling form. However, its capacity to manage many of its new (and old) tasks has been seriously limited by the financial and political constraints placed upon it since the late 1970s. The contradiction at the heart of the role of social work in managing the crisis lies in the fact that it has been expected to respond to pressures for a more robust approach to many contemporary problems when it has been so comprehensively identified as part of the problem itself, one of the factors contributing to the crisis in the first place. Social work has had to struggle for legitimacy as an indispensable part of the state's response to contemporary social problems; it has had to fight a rearguard action against attacks on its efficiency while simultaneously developing new strategies to manage the ever increasing range of priorities.

The police have never been the subject of such a protracted and concentrated pillorying as social work, although, as we have suggested, they have not escaped criticism in recent years. To some extent the police have been victims of their own rhetoric in claiming that an increased investment in police resources would pay off in reduced rates of crime. This has manifestly failed to occur. There has been a marked shift in emphasis in the way the police now present the crime problem, away from an emphasis on their own individual role toward a strategy which emphasises the contribution which the communities themselves and other agencies can play in fighting crime. The 'multi-agency' approach has become the fashionable motif adorning new initiatives in the crime and crime-related fields. It signals a lack of faith amongst managers of state agencies in their own capacities to manage an increasingly complex array of social problems. The multi-agency approach provides a new solution at a time when public confidence in powerful agencies to resolve the crime problem is ebbing away. For managers of all agencies, the approach also promises to increase their control over rank-and-file workers who consistently defy attempts to regulate and control their behaviour. Now, instead of talking to dissident and unmanageable workers, the managers can talk, or engage in constructive dialogue, with each other; the multi-agency approach provides a language for communication between senior personnel who frequently have more in common with each other than with the junior members of their own occupational cultures. An important dimension of the eruption of interest in multi-agency work is the opportunity it affords to cement relationships between managers at senior level. Indeed, as we shall demonstrate, this aspect frequently becomes the primary goal of multi-agency work, where it expands the spheres of interest of senior personnel into new areas. This may increase the status of these 'new professionals' and provide at least the illusion that they are controlling events, but this approach may be treated with suspicion or derision by lower-level workers, for whom it involves co-operation with people generally believed to be hostile and untrustworthy outsiders.

Whatever the problems multi-agency work creates for agencies, the rhetoric of 'working together' has gripped the imaginations of senior professionals and policy-makers. Since the early 1980s there have been numerous policy statements which place inter-agency co-operation at the centre of a new approach. Innovations in fields as diverse as juvenile liaison, drug control, crime prevention and child protection have been designed around a joint approach to these problems: no innovation would be complete without its obligatory reference to the need for shared work and genuine co-operation. In the crime prevention field the approach involved the co-ordination of agencies such as the police, social services and housing as well as an increased sensitivity to local crime problems (in general the approach has gone along with an interest in gauging specifically local needs and characteristics). This objective was clearly stated in the Home Office Circular 8/84, which stands as a clear example of official faith in multi-agency work. It claimed that 'crime prevention schemes are more successful where the police and other agencies work together in a coordinated way toward particular aims', and, since patterns of crime vary, 'preventive measures are therefore more likely to be successful when designed to reflect local characteristics and focussed on particular types of crime'.

The belief that a joint approach to such problems will bear fruit in this way has not always been well founded. Nevertheless, the belief in the joint approach as a 'good thing' in itself continues to exert a powerful influence on official thinking. One example of this influence is provided by a crime prevention experiment on an estate in Rochdale, Greater Manchester, which set out to reduce burglaries by a co-ordinated strategy. It was found that the two things did not go hand in hand. The report on the project reflects on a lack of enthusiasm on the part of some agencies to participate and a consequent uncertainty about whether the scheme should continue regardless. The authors recall their uncertainty:

... the priority of the two aims were often in tension. On the one hand following 8/84, we aspired to establish robust links between agencies so that in the long term crime prevention would be effective. On the other hand we wished to show quickly that it was possible to prevent some crime of a kind thought to be intractable . . . Ideally we wished to do both, but we often wondered which we should strive for as a priority. (Forrester *et al*, 1988, p 1).

After consultation with the Home Office it was decided to pursue the aim of reducing burglary even though this meant relying on only one agency working alone. This extract illustrates the extent to which inter-agency co-operation can become a powerful definer of the aims of projects even when it produces no tangible benefits. The scheme was very successful in reducing burglaries on the estate, but those responsible were almost embarrassed that it managed to do so without some complex inter-agency machinery.

Other areas have similarly been subjected to calls for a more integrated approach. The Research and Planning Unit of the Home Office has been influential in providing a rationale and an agenda for inter-agency work in the crime field. The selection of papers under the heading *Managing Criminal Justice* (Moxon, 1985) encourages the police and social workers to think of criminal justice as an integrated system rather than as a series of disconnected institutions. Each agency should be encouraged to think about the inter-connectedness of its activities with other agencies and with the system as a whole. This kind of thinking was influential in defining the agenda in initiatives in juvenile liaison which have emerged since the early 1980s. The Northamptonshire juvenile liaison bureaux were explicitly established on an inter-agency basis with seconded representatives of the major agencies responsible for juveniles in the county. There is some dispute about whether such initiatives have increased diversion from prosecution and shielded young people from the labelling process, or have intensified the capacity of the state to widen the net and control young people by less formal means (a question discussed in greater detail in Chapter 6).

Criminologists have responded to the emergence of multi-agency work with either dismay or approval, depending largely, though not exclusively, on their political orientation. Some have embraced the notion as the way to manage rationally the complexities of modern society, while others have detected an authoritarian aspect to the process. Simon Holdaway (1986) and Terry Thomas (1986) have been among the most enthusiastic advocates of a multi-agency approach as a means of overcoming differences in professional culture which place an obstacle in the way of the realisation of what are essentially shared goals. Hence Holdaway urges social workers and police officers to come together on the basis of 'shared uncertainties', rather than go on hiding behind the fortifications of occupational cultures.

Both Holdaway and Thomas emphasise the degree of similarity in the problems social workers and police officers face, and argue for increased negotiation to arrive at a consensus. Others have taken an optimistic stance in relation to the potential for improving the quality of life for people in the inner city via increased multi-agency work. The 'left realist' school in particular have called for a multi-agency approach to resolve the crisis in areas of high social tension and crime (Lea *et al*, 1986, Lea *et al*, 1987), and the approach is advocated by those concerned with the aftermath of the urban disturbances in British cities (Gifford, 1986). In their analysis of multi-agency work and locally based crime initiatives, Sampson *et al* (1988) refer to this advocacy of multi-agency work as the 'benevolent' approach to the crime problem and to local agencies. It is underpinned by a view of both local communities and local agencies as fairly homogeneous units, sharing a core set of values and beliefs, despite superficial differences. Sampson *et al* also identify what they call a 'conspiratorial model' of agency practice. This approach sees multi-agency work as a police-led strategy designed to 'take over' other agencies and use them for its own ends. The multi-agency approach becomes a way in which problem communities can be more effectively policed and coerced; multi-agency work can increase the flow of information available to the police and provide a form of surveillance. Paul Gordon, in his critique of community policing, argues that the multi-agency approach provides the police with opportunities to 'penetrate' communities and 'break down resistance' (Gordon, 1984, p 50), by using other agencies to gain 'access to areas, communities and information which could otherwise not be available to them'. A similar message is given by Phil Scraton, who sees multi-agency work as part of a process of expanding the control of society by the police; a form of 'total policing' (Scraton, 1985, p 139). The 'conspiratorial' model views the emergence of the multi-agency approach as part of a general project of increasing coercion by the state, which is rapidly shedding its commitment to welfare and infiltrating further into civil society (in line with Stanley Cohen's thesis (1985). The multi-agency approach would fit into a model of increased 'statism' outlined by Poulantzas:

> The doors of the old control sites are 'opening' to give way to a new type of statism; that of more flexible networks and circuits spread through the social fabric . . . this process involves a lifting of the traditional boundaries between the normal and the abnormal . . . thus, control is shifted from the criminal act to the crime inducing situation, from the pathological case to the pathogenic surroundings, in such a way that each citizen becomes, as it were, an a priori suspect or a potential criminal (Poulantzas, 1978, pp 186–7).

Conspiracy theories of the state inevitably tend to overestimate the degree of consensus within state apparatuses and to perceive the state as a monolithic body without internal contradictions. The 'benevolent' perspective has no theory of state power at all. The state is seen as a conglomeration of institutions without any real internal structure and purpose. This view conforms to the traditional social democratic tendency to see the state as a neutral piece of machinery that reformers can take over and direct to their own ends, whereas the conspiracy model tends to see the state as representing the interests of the ruling class. There are significant points of difference between these two models, but there are also some notable points of similarity. Both perspectives, for very different reasons, tend to undervalue the degree of conflict and differentiation within communities. The conspiracy thesis tends to see communities as relatively homogeneous units based upon shared class interests, whereas the benevolent thesis is inclined to see communities as homogeneous units based upon a core of commonly held values and beliefs. Traditional Marxist theory, from which the conspiracy model is largely derived, has always tended to see communities in class terms and underestimated the divisions within communities based upon such factors as race, gender and age: communities are places to which the working class goes when it is not working. On the other hand the benevolent perspective tends to overestimate the degree of cohesiveness within communities because of its belief in the primacy of ties based upon family and neighbourhood.

The limits and possibilities of multi-agency work

Neither of these positions adequately grasps the complexities of multi-agency work, of the state generally, or of the internal composition of communities. These require a more nuanced approach which is sensitive to the various factors governing the emergence of multi-agency work and how it affects communities. Multi-agency work is not an unproblematic, conflict-free solution to the problems of modern society, but neither is it simply another stage in the expansion of the monolithic state. Gordon (1984) and others view its development as an indication of police confidence: a means of further extending their power by colonising other agencies, and thereby increasing their power over communities. We would suggest that the emergence of multi-agency initiatives could just as easily be seen as representing a loss of confidence by the police and the exhaustion of their crime-fighting strategy. It may be less a sign of confidence than an admission that their belief in their own omnipotence was misplaced.

Multi-agency work has been placed on the agenda at the same time as increased pressure on the police to start showing a return for the resources invested in them since the late 1970s; pressure was growing, too, for improvements in their response to the forms of victimisation outlined above. The conspiracy model undervalues the impact which pressure from society has had on state agencies and the capacity for reform within these agencies. On the other hand, the relationships between agencies are not conflict-free, nor do agencies share power equally. Some are clearly more powerful than others. The police do have a tendency to set the agenda upon which negotiations between agencies are based, and thus to shape the form of agency liaison. This does not mean that they simply take other agencies over wholesale; there is resistance and struggle within inter-agency bodies, some of which are successful in challenging the police's definitions of how the body should be run. The juvenile liaison schemes in Northampton-shire were developed on the basis of a consensus about the need to divert juveniles from the courts; but the bureaux had constantly to struggle with the police over the number of cautions a juvenile could actually receive before a court disposal would become automatic; and they were often successful in doing so. Similarly, some locally based crime prevention panels (which involve bodies such as NACRO as well as statutory agencies) have been successful in challenging the police's definition of crime prevention as a simple matter of 'nuts, bolts and window locks', and have developed more socially based alternatives. In one instance, noted by Sampson *et al* (1988), a Victim Support Scheme on a London estate actually improved its services to victims following a conflict between the police and other agencies when this led to referrals being processed through channels other than the police. This conflict was also influential in challenging police stereotypes of who were 'deserving' and 'undeserving' victims.

Relationships between agencies generally are marked by conflict and tension rather than by consensus and unity. This may not be altogether a bad thing. While the benevolent model sees harmonious relationships as a prerequisite for improved services to the commun-ity, too close or cosy a relationship between agencies may actually harm communities and client groups. Professional relationships based upon confidentiality and trust may also be jeopardised, when workers share information with other agencies. In our research we have seen situations develop in which juvenile liaison panels engage in gratuitous gossip about particular children which, while having no bearing on the particular offence under discussion, tended to estab-lish the child as a 'problem' for the agencies and make him or her 'someone to be watched'. We were disturbed by the amount of time which was spent sharing stories about particular families who were a common problem for the agencies (in this case the police, social ser-vices, probation and education), which confirmed that they should be labelled as deviant or pathological: here good relations were bought at the expense of vulnerable groups of people. Generally when agencies share a common perception of a problem, and when this remains unchallenged, they feel less inclined to seek clarification from other sources than their own professional certainty.

We have seen situations in which such certainty has had disastrous repercussions. Saxon Lane, part of a Lancashire town studied during research on multi-agency work, was considered by all the agencies to be a 'problem estate', because of the high rates of crime and other social factors. Although such a view was not actually borne out by the crime rates or other social problem indicators, the estate became the recipient of a joint agency action designed to tackle its underlying problems. The crime problem on the estate was 'talked up' by senior members of the police and housing department as a means of attracting funds for a major crime prevention programme: a brief mêlée outside a fish-and-chip shop became a 'riot'. The programme, once established, did have benefits for some residents who had doors and windows replaced or repaired, and new locks fitted. On the other hand the emphasis on crime in the neighbourhood strengthened the image of the estate as being an 'estate of fear'. Thus the reputation of the estate declined rather than improved as the crime emphasis tended to add to the adverse public and official labelling. One consequence of this was further to erode confidence in the locality as somewhere safe and desirable to live. Residents on the estate and those adjoining it began to send their children to schools some distance away in order to avoid stigmatisation. The local school, which had been trying to establish itself as a much needed community resource on the estate, suffered a dramatic decline in rolls and was closed down.

This example demonstrates the problems inherent in shared perceptions of a particular problem, particularly when it is regarded as a question of crime. The example also inverts the 'broken windows' thesis of Wilson and Kelling (1982), because it was the very emphasis on crime on the estate (which for them would be a strategy for saving neighbourhoods) which further damaged the estate and accelerated the decline. It also shows the dangers of seeing community problems purely in terms of crime and overestimating the impact particular sorts of crime have on neighbourhood integration, *à lá* Wilson and Kelling. On this particular estate community integration could actually be said to have improved as the result of some crime: some very successful 'stolen goods' parties were said to have taken place there, and fixing gas meters to run at no cost to the consumer, provided local employment, as did other features of the 'hidden' economy. There are other ways in which an emphasis on crime in police-led inter-agency bodies can have dangerous unintended consequences and become the sources of further problems for residents. Sampson *et al* (1988) provide an example from an estate in London, on which heavy security doors with electronic card-key devices were placed on walk-ways, in an effort to prevent skate-boarding young-sters from marauding along them and snatching handbags. The elderly on the estate found these devices impossible to operate and became trapped in a steel fortress, isolated from friends and neighbours.

There may be important professional reasons why police officers and social workers are preoccupied with different tasks and problems and see their resolution in different terms. We have already estab-lished that some conflict on the basis of these different preoccupa-tions can actually be beneficial and improve services. Social workers in particular may have to resist strong pressures from the police to dictate the agenda for liaison. Given what has been called the 'struc-tural subordination' of social work to the policies and practices of other, more powerful agencies (Clarke *et al*, 1980), this is not always an easy task to accomplish. Social work's own crisis of legitimacy has placed it in a position where it may seek to become involved with pro-jects that have the consent of other agencies as a means of deflecting criticism. We should like to argue that social work should become involved with inter-agency initiatives which are clearly aimed at improving services for clients and for communities, especially when these initiatives attempt to incorporate the interests of client groups and actively involve communities.

Inter-agency bodies seem to work best when they have a clear pur-pose in mind and are focussing upon a specific task, rather than when they are just more general 'talking shops'. These may make profes-sionals feel better about each other, but do little to help anyone else: too often schemes are deemed a success simply because of the improved relations between officials. Care must also be taken that liaison does not compromise professional roles and boundaries, or that one agency is not simply being recruited to rubber-stamp the unmodified practices or another, more powerful agency – a tendency we have found in several juvenile liaison panels. In such situations professionals from weaker agencies may feel compelled to go along with unpalatable decisions for fear of 'rocking the boat', or damaging relationships which have been deemed necessary for political reasons at the senior level. On the other hand, we have observed instances where multi-agency agreements, formulated at the senior level, are effectively 'sabotaged' on the ground by subordinates, who refuse to accept the need to co-ordinate their activities with workers to whom they are implacably hostile. More commonly, though, the rhetoric of liaison proves impossible to put into practice because of the vague-ness of liaison agreements drawn up by the senior staff; they tend to dwell on the principle of co-operation and leave issues of implement-ation unclear. The Home Beat Officers who worked from the joint agency based on Saxon Lane were supposed to co-ordinate their work with other professionals on the estate, although no one told them so (until we did): one police officer called this the 'mushroom principle' of management: 'they leave us in the dark and feed us shit'.

Developing useful multi-agency work may also depend upon genuine consultation with groups and bodies outside the state. This, while often being recognised in theories of policy, is difficult to implement in practice: professionals have enough difficulty in talking to one another, let alone to non-professionals outside the statutory sector. Where they do attempt to liaise with community organisations, as for instance in police community liaison, they tend to be very selective about which groups they consider to be 'representative'. There is also a tendency to see consultation and 'information sharing' as a one-way process (Blagg *et al*, 1988). Agencies may use communities and voluntary groups as a means of gauging opinion, as an additional source of referral, or as somewhere to refer cases on to (one volunteer working on a community-based programme for juveniles in London called this being used as a 'dustbin for their rubbish work').

This negative comment apart, there have been some positive developments in the use of voluntary bodies to undertake work alongside statutory agencies. The National Association of Victim Support Schemes is an obvious example of a voluntary agency which takes referrals from statutory agencies, mainly the police, and has been generally regarded as a welcome innovation by researchers (Maguire and Corbett, 1987). In other areas the needs of particular client groups and sections of the community may demand a greater degree of influence by these groups on the actual practices of agencies. The problem of racism within statutory agencies can only be changed, Dominelli has argued, by allowing black people to criticise, challenge and effectively monitor the practice and orientation of social workers in their work with black people (Dominelli, 1988). Similarly, while the police and social services have not been averse to using women's refuges, rape crisis centres and other such bodies as a means of coping with some of the problems they face in dealing with sexual and other forms of violence within families, they may not wish to allow these bodies to challenge their overall patterns of work.

In this chapter we have outlined some important themes in the debates about crime, communities and multi-agency work. We have attempted to place these themes within the shifting landscape of contemporary Britain. In presenting the issues in this way we may be accused of neglecting other important features of the current crisis. We recognise that the concern about street crime and public disorder has involved white youth as well as black, almost exclusively so in the context of 'football hooliganism'. We do not wish to minimise such issues; but we have attempted to raise others, principally those centred on race and gender, which have often been neglected by observers of crime problems. These issues, we would argue, have an autonomous existence as crucial features of the present policy and policing scene, and are not simply manifestations of an ongoing conflict between the working class and the state.

Crime, we have suggested, is too vast and complex a phenomenon to be easily monopolised for very long by any one political bloc, but is the subject of constant redefinition and reformulation, as new themes emerge and, with them, new pressures for change. The emergence of multi-agency work reflects a growing unease about one particular solution to the crime problem: that of policing. Whatever the dangers for social work in becoming involved in multi-agency work – and we do not underrate them – the fact that it has been increasingly drawn into work with other agencies reveals that social work cannot be simply dismissed as an anachronistic hang-over from the 'permissive 60s', but is an integral, perhaps indispensable, part of any contemporary strategy in the fields of crime and related problems.

3 Problems of youth social work: themes and innovations

No debate about post-war conceptions of the crime problem would be complete without some reference to the issue of youth. In Chapters 5 and 6 we outline current philosophy and practice in social work with young offenders. Before doing so we wish to identify some common problems in youth social work shared by young people in the wider community. *Rethinking Youth Social Work* (Paley *et al*, 1986) and other such initiatives, have been attempts to redefine the aims of youth-orientated social work, in ways which take account of many contemporary concerns – concerns about the problems young people face in the modern city as well as the more obvious concern to minimise the damage the young people themselves do to others and to their surroundings. As we have already suggested there is a dangerous dimension to forms of crime prevention which attempt a 'situational' solution to crime problems. As with black people, there is a tendency to see young people as *a priori* suspects in the community. We have illustrated the ways in which making the environment crime-proof can seriously undermine the ability of certain groups, the young and the old, to move about freely. In this chapter we wish to demonstrate how a 'social approach' to crime prevention can overcome the problems posed by the 'situational' approach. First, we illustrate some of the ways policing 'social space' can actually socially disenfranchise young people and in particular black youth by denying them equal access to the 'public arena' of society.

Within the mainstream of the youth service there are debates going on concerning the future development of its work. Some of this debate reflects a desire to get back in touch with grass-roots developments. Youth workers we have contacted fear that the service has become too specialised, concerned with specific client groups rather than with young people in general. Others are concerned with finding ways of working with 'at risk' groups that do not lead to labelling. This has been reflected in recent publications (Paley *et al*, 1986;

John, 1986; Smith, 1987) and the message seems to be one of cautious encouragement for forms of preventative work with at-risk groups – rather than individuals – as long as 'at risk' is not used as a judgement imposed for moral or psychological reasons:

> ... 'at risk' and 'in trouble' are not adjectives which ascribe qualities to individuals; rather, they are prepositional phrases which refer to situations in which people are apt to find themselves. To say someone is 'at risk' or 'in trouble' is to say no more about what sort of person they are than to say they are 'at' the sea side or 'in' Blackpool (Paley *et al*, p 4).

This view point typifies the position adopted in the three publications mentioned above. Basically it is that youth work should be about meeting the needs of young people generally rather than explicitly targeting crime as the single most important concern.

One of the areas of concern for the National Youth Bureau (and it is a recurrent theme in this research) is the position of intermediate treatment in social crime prevention work. The problem is to some extent an historical one. Following the 1969 Children and Young Persons Act, IT was initially seen as a youth service activity and a community resource, but while this conception of it has remained a policy commitment, it has in reality been suppressed in favour of strategies designed to handle offenders. This process has been further advanced by the LAC 83 (3) initiative (discussed in Chapter 6), which funded voluntary associations to establish alternatives to custody projects in conjunction with local authorities. (It is possible to overstate the extent to which this process is complete and uniform, as the example of Scotland will show.) This new 'orthodoxy' of IT development also overlooks the degree of boundary-blurring possible with inter-agency work and the success which the IT schemes have had in setting up specialist units such as girls' groups, etc (the ideologically 'purest' models tend to remain in the arena funded by LAC 83 (3)). Errol John has argued that IT should continue to be identified with 'known offenders' whereas work with those 'on the threshold of care' or preventative work should be called youth work or youth social work (John, 1986). Before we outline in detail this social approach we first need to establish some of the features of this change that has taken place in the social environment. Processes of urban redevelopment and economic changes have affected the ways in which young people relate to the urban environment. These changes have transformed patterns of leisure and the ways in which young people use social space; these new social spaces are being policed in ways which can adversely affect the ability of young people to enjoy access to them on an equal basis with other members of society. This is because access to this social space is increasingly a function of one's position as a consumer (although other criteria such as race may also be a factor); and the forms of policing employed in these settings, particularly with the dramatic expansion of private policing in this country, have created particular difficulties for the young. This is not just a feature of traditional 'inner city' Britain but has infiltrated into new towns and suburban Britain as well.

Case study I: Midtown

We shall pursue these themes with reference to two particular case studies. 'Midtown' in the East Midlands is an example of a city which was hit by the closure of its main industry, a steel works, in the early 1980s. This coincided with the creation of a new city centre, a 'shopping mall' along American lines policed by a Praetorian Guard of private security men. Midtown is an interesting example because of its strongly entrenched working-class culture, a culture transplanted from the Clyde in the 1950s and 1960s; as a case study it reveals some of the tensions between traditional working-class cultures and the new culture of consumerism.

In this research a cohort of 35 young people (15 girls : 20 boys) were interviewed over a lengthy period and the interviews were supplemented by accompanying them on their travels through Midtown. Their overall feeling was that Midtown was 'dead', 'boring', 'a hole'. They were also deeply pessimistic about the future; the traditional option of the steelworks, with its predictable avenues to assimilation into adult world was no longer open to them, and they tended to be dubious about the reality of the 'economic miracle' that was supposedly taking off around them. (It had been rumoured that the town was to be revived by the opening of a 'Disneyworld': a prospect treated rather sceptically by many of the youths.) One social worker said that Midtown's unusual position – an outpost of Scotland set in a hostile sea of East Midlands market towns – made it feel incredibly claustrophobic for the young in particular; it was, he said, 'like living in an open prison'. The decline in the steel industry was also affecting the overall texture of family life in Midtown. The research involved gauging the patterns of continuity and change between the inherited culture of the Clyde and the lived reality of life in a new, though economically unstable, town.

'Jimmy' had worked as a lorry driver in the steelworks. He believed that the closure of the steelworks had all but killed a way of life:

> . . . when the steelworks went bust it killed this place off. People came here to get away from . . . a poor life. But now what will men do? The older ones will never get jobs now. . . . The young ones are dissatisfied.

Jimmy did not think that unemployment caused crime directly, but like many of the adults contacted he believed that the 'consumer society' created a promise it could not fulfil for the young unemployed. It was affecting the young ones too, who believed it a waste of time to work hard at school. His feelings about the break-up of working-class solidarity of the kind he had known in Glasgow were reflected in other interviews with adults. Their accounts – though tinged with nostalgia – were realistic about many of the drawbacks of Glasgow life. Jimmy had grown up in the Blackhill area of Glasgow.

> Jimmy: Well, you've got your next door neighbour here but it's not the same . . . if you're short of a cup of sugar in Glasgow you go to the chap next door, he'll say aye sure . . . you can't do that here. There is a kind o' community here, just not as deep. In Glasgow there would be 20 or 30 kids all playing together – here they've all got their own gardens and front doors to play around . . .

Jimmy etched vividly a changed cultural landscape, a world at once more privatised and differentiated, less focused on the neighbourhood as a source of entertainment and support. In other important ways too the combination of modern life-styles and economic change was affecting social life. The new light industries did not seem to be a part of the town in the way the old steelworks had been. Like many new features of the economy, their relationship to the social space they occupy borders on indifference. John Urry has called this phenomenon the ability to 'transcend the city' (Urry, 1985, p 33); a capacity made possible by the development of multi-plant enterprises integrated and controlled on a national rather than a local basis, the locality being only a 'labour pool' (p 35), rather than an integral unit in the production and reproduction of capital. The precise implications of this process for relationships within civil society form the subject of intense debate (see the essays in Gregory and Urry, 1985) and we do not intend to dwell on them here. There were, though, some quite discernible changes taking place, not only in the more obvious sphere of employment opportunities in Midtown, but also in the orientation of young people towards their locality and the wider social spaces in general – which, rather like the economic processes noted by Urry and others, were being modified and adapted in novel ways.

The movements of the young people were far more diverse than just playing on those 'old mean streets' of their neighbourhoods. Only the very young routinely and habitually focused on the street as a place for 'mucking about'; the older youths took in quite an expansive social and geographic spread for their leisure which now included the city centre as a place to congregate. Their day would include not only the obvious and fixed points of home and school, but also some rather fluid and negotiated use of public arenas and youth facilities. It was surprising how quickly a youth club, for example, would become 'boring' and useless as a source of entertainment; it was not that there were not enough of these places, rather that, after an initial period of novelty, they would just become like everywhere else: 'boring!'. Moreover, the local youth clubs operated by strict codes of behaviour: young people who 'caused trouble', or who were known to have been in trouble with the police, were frequently barred from using the facilities.

The city centre was an important focus for activity, or just 'doing nothing' (Corrigan, 1979), of course. This is not really surprising, 'What better place,' Paul Willis argues, 'to express the longings of a frustrated consumerism,' than in that 'mecca of images', the shopping centre? (Willis, 1984). Shopping areas such as Midtown's have become an established feature of the refurbished city centre and they attract youth like magnets. The older boys and girls in particular see the shopping centre as an integral part of their social scene. The youth of Midtown admitted that they and their friends had indulged in some occasional shop-lifting, although they also felt they were treated unnecessarily harshly by shopkeepers and especially by the private security police.

> Darren: We are always getting hassled by the police . . . you are just standing there with your mates, yeh? . . . and they come along and just push you about . . . and say f . . . off home or I'll do ya.
> Will: Aye, and it's worse in the shops, they have people following you about . . . watching you all the time. We're always being kicked out of shops. Everyone thinks you're a criminal.

If the current trend towards shopping precincts based on the American 'mall' continues, then it is possible to foresee increasing difficulties for young people, especially the unemployed young adults, unless some kind of provision for youth can be incorporated in the precinct which is more satisfying than the computerised 'penny arcades' in which many young people congregate. There is a real problem here. Cities are not open spaces to which everyone can enjoy equal access, but are instead becoming segregated and polarised into 'radically antagonistic spaces' (Berman, 1981). Mike Davis illustrates this process as it has unfolded in the United States of America, where city centres have become 'a problematic area':

> Genuine public spaces, whether as parks, streets, places of entertainment, or in urban transport were devalued as amenities and redefined as planning problems to be eliminated or privatised (Davis, 1985).

The 'elite urban pastoralism' of the little malls and arcades represents for Davis a 'profoundly anti-urban impulse', and it resolves the dilemma faced by middle-class white Americans who can indulge in consumerism without the problems of the street. The increasing tendency to separate out 'the street' (the term itself having become a powerful metaphor for danger) as a universal thoroughfare from the process of buying and selling raises dilemmas for the young – a process only exacerbated by the increased use of private security firms to police the malls, a form of policing which generally means evicting 'undesirables'. For where 'tacit norms' have evolved to resolve difficulties between working-class youth and the police on the local street (Cohen, 1979), extra difficulties are presented by the growth of 'privatised' realms in which youths with little money have no business at all. It is clear that some forms of crime prevention, which seem explicitly to target youths as suspects, play a role in further segregating and ghettoising social space in a manner detrimental to the needs of the young.

The Midtown example reveals some of the problems young people face in negotiating the changing urban environment. We have already established that the issue of racism creates a further range of problems. Youth-related forms of social work are frequently at the centre of conflicts emanating from these various problems. What role can and should they play in resolving tensions between young people and authority and on whose side should they be in the conflicts between different youth groups? The various traditional models of work do not provide blueprints for intervention in these areas: youth work has become focused on clubs, not public space; IT on the 'system', social work on the family, education (obviously) on schools. Young people, however, do not live their lives conveniently parcelled up into any one of these neat institutional boundaries; and it is often in the spaces between them that the young are at their most vulnerable, and most dangerous to others. When faced with situations that they cannot locate within their domains many professionals become paralysed and unable to act. One brief example of this problem: a woman social worker told us of a case where some girls she knew were being sexually abused by a group of older boys in the same neighbourhood. These boys were known to the local IT officers, having been on IT orders for offending. She approached the IT workers, as they knew the boys well, and asked them to intervene. The IT workers refused – their job was to keep boys like these 'out of the system' and her request smacked of the kind of discredited 'preventive' IT and would only serve to widen the net of 'the system'. Within the limits of their own definition of their work the IT workers could maintain that this was not their problem; others might suggest that they were hiding behind their own professional codes of practice in order not to become involved in a potentially messy and difficult situation.

Youth social work has increasingly had to confront situations which constantly challenge its capacity to remain impartial when young people become involved with crime or become victims of criminal behaviour. We shall illustrate below some of the ways in which some youth workers are attempting to build appropriate strategies.

First we shall provide another case study, which illustrates some key problems for youth work. It is an important one because it covers many of the themes we have already identified as key sources of uncertainty.

Case study II: Oldtown

Oldtown is a district in a north-eastern town (Milltown) which is mainly inhabited by people of Asian origin. It has suffered from long-term neglect, and its old housing-stock of mainly privately rented accommodation has had little attention from the local Labour council. The feeling on this estate was that they were ignored by local politicians and local agencies – in particular they felt that the Labour council took their votes for granted, acquiring redevelopment funds from central government by emphasising the problems of Oldtown and then channelling these funds into developments in the city centre and on white estates. At the very heart of the Oldtown area is a community centre, which we shall call Cannon Street; this centre housed a youth club, which was attended by many of the local Asian youth. The centre saw itself as a 'multi-ethnic' institution, catering for all sections of the community, and the staff were mainly white with few Asians occupying positions of power. (It was argued by the white staff that because the centre housed both Pakistani and Indian welfare associations, whites had to occupy a leading position in order to prevent conflict between these supposedly rival factions.) The staff saw their role as 'honest brokers' not only between different factions on the estate but also between people on the estate and local agencies: this 'neutrality' was called into question, however, when tensions emerged between radicalised sections of black youth and the local agencies.

During 1987 the police voiced concern about what they saw as an escalating problem of 'youth gang fights'. Although these were often between black and white youth the police did not regard them as racial, but rather as traditional conflicts over territory. This view was to some extent shared by the workers at Cannon Street, and by representatives of other statutory and voluntary agencies interviewed by us in the town. Indeed there was a remarkable degree of consensus about the problem, which included also the local leaders of the Asian community. Althought the community police officer on the estate recognised that there was a problem of racial prejudice locally he was of the opinion that the conflict was mainly about territory:

> This has been designated a sensitive area . . . one must be aware all the time of racial attacks and racial motives . . . I think that attacks recently are not racially motivated . . . a lot of it is literally 'hot blood'. . . . The youth are fighting for territory. They say, 'this is our territory and we are going to defend it' . . . they don't have any confidence in the police and they have to defend it from people from outside.

For the Cannon Street staff, the 'gang fights' created some real dilemmas. Although they believed that racism was a problem, they too accepted that much of the conflict was territorial rather than racial. Moreover, the increasing radicalism of the black youth was creating problems for their position as a neutral, multi-racial body. The centre was being appropriated by the youth on the estate as a part of their territory and there was unease at the prospect of the centre coming to be regarded as a black organisation, particularly a radical black one. The youth themselves felt betrayed by the centre and by their own community elders as well, victims of racism by the police (though not by the local community policeman mentioned above, whom they respected but who they felt was ineffectual in defending them) as well as by many whites. There were two particular aspects of white racism about which they felt particularly angry: firstly, they felt excluded from equal access to the city itself (unlike the Midtown example this was not a simple issue of being heavily policed, they were subjected to racist abuse). Secondly, they felt that the police were turning a blind eye to increasing invasions of their locality by racist white youth.

The centre director said:

> ... some [fighting] is racially motivated ... some racially motivated crimes ... some 'tit for tat' fighting. The young are becoming protective about what they see as their territory ... I'm a bit worried, it's [Cannon Street] being seen as a black youth club but that wasn't the intention. The blacks are saying we will look after our own. ... The youth get together when they see large numbers of white youths and they see the police disperse them while protecting the whites. We have real problems and they are getting worse. People are making a stand. They see the police as unable to do anything about it.

This particular worker still believed that it was territory rather than race that was at stake in the conflict, a view shared by other workers in the centre and by the police at large. It was also shared by many of the older inhabitants of Oldtown who had been born on the Indian subcontinent, particularly by their religious and political leaders.

The 'interests' of the Asian community were represented by an alliance of mosque leaders and members of the local council Labour party leadership in Milltown: the Labour leadership had close links with Cannon Street via a number of workers who mixed various forms of ethnic relations and youth work with Labour politics. The youth in particular were not only resentful of the Cannon Street set-up but were also frustrated by the position of the community elders and what they felt was a continuous accommodation with the local white political power. They were also concerned with what they perceived as an increased problem of racism locally, manifesting itself in the increased confidence of white racist youth in coming into the area and the increasing difficulties for black youth going into town. A group – known locally as the BMWs (Black Muslim Warriors) – had been actively defending the locality against incursions by white youth who, it was believed, enjoyed the protection of the police. In their opinion there had been an increase in the amount of racial harassment in Oldtown which was ignored by the police.

> The young people are not prepared to put up with this indefinitely . . . you can't know how angry they are. . . . The milk crates and the petrol are ready – one day this place will go up in flames like Toxteth.'

The black youths felt that people of their parents' generation tended to accept the 'ethnicity' divide and had accommodated themselves to the limits placed on them by this. It meant, amongst other things, an acceptance that 'they' were 'Asian' first and foremost. This was seen as common sense by many people, including the community and mosque leaders who had a particular economic and political stake in the community retaining its 'cultural identity'. These leaders had various ties with local Labour leaders who in turn had closer links with agencies such as Cannon Street. The older generation were, it was said, content to make a bit of money and perhaps even return 'home' at some stage. One young man, frustrated with Cannon Street, and angry at what he saw as police collusion with racism, went to see a community/mosque leader to enlist his support:

> He said to me, 'look here, we have to accept that we are in a foreign country, just try to keep your head down and make some money, that's all we are here for'. I was stunned.

The youth believed that black people should enjoy the same rights of access to public spaces as white people and became incensed by the ways in which these spaces were closed off to them: the city centre was considered to be beyond their territory:

> . . . we were getting sick of being hassled in town, we are not allowed in the clubs, they say 'we don't want any trouble, so go back to your own side' and we are always the first to be thrown out. You daren't even look at a white girl.

The black youths also claimed that they had to take the blame when there was any trouble in town and yet they had to suffer all kinds of racial abuse from white people as a matter of course. Many of the boys could no longer bear to walk into the centre of town with their parents because they could not stand to see their parents humiliated before their eyes by racist remarks. One young man went to see the leader of the community relations council, another Labour councillor: 'I told him about the trouble we had going into town and he said, "well don't go then"!'

Further signs of racism were interpreted as symptoms of youth aggression rather than as racial attacks. The black youth began to resist what they saw as deliberate attempts to enter the Oldtown area by white racist youth; some ugly incidents occurred. Police set up the Group Disorder Team or 'Gang Busters' to respond to what they saw as an increased problem of youth gang fights. Arrests were made following incidents when whites went into Oldtown. The blacks believed that they were picked on by the police and arrested, while white youth were set free, and that they were treated less favourably in court. The black youth felt particularly betrayed when the leadership of the Cannon Street centre seemed to side with the police – indeed, sat with them – at a 'clear the air' meeting arranged by local politicians. Since then many of them have boycotted the centre and campaigned for a new leadership representing their interests. The racial situation on the estate continues to deteriorate.

This example illustrates the range of difficulties and social tensions with which youth social work is increasingly having to contend. These antagonisms reflect tensions in our society and forms of oppression which cannot be resolved by any one agency acting in isolation, nor can they be resolved by forms of intervention by professionals 'from above'. In the previous chapter we have detailed some criticisms of the multi-agency approach as it is presently perceived. There are, though, other models of inter-agency co-operation which can deal more effectively with these problems at the grass-roots, and some of them are becoming influential in locally based strategies which take as their focus not just 'crime' as it is defined and given priority by powerful agencies but also many of the underlying social problems which create crime, and some social issues which often do not become priorities for powerful agencies. We have identified two contemporary areas of concern in this chapter, those of 'loss of citizenship' or 'disenfranchisement', and racism. In the case of racism, and in the example of the IT workers who refused to intervene with boys who were sexually abusing young girls, the problem is particularly difficult for some youth professionals to deal with because they are being asked to make a choice between 'different' youth groups. All young people are to a large degree powerless, yet some are quite clearly less powerful than others. The autonomy of white youth in Milltown was to some extent at the expense of the local black youth: they could gain a spurious kind of citizenship through their association with their 'Britishness', and join the 'imagined' community, something the black youth were not permitted to do. Ironically, their problem was not that they refused to 'integrate' and 'assimilate' – rather that they were refused assimilation on equal terms.

The 'normal process of maturation in the community' which may commentators see as the route out of delinquency (Rutherford, 1986) is not without problems. 'Normal maturation' may imply a tacit legitimation of forms of subjugation of girls and women in a community where the oppression of women is considered natural; the way boys become men. This may seem a harsh judgement on IT. However, we should like to argue, and we are by no means alone in this (Stubbs, 1988a; Hudson, 1988), that agencies should be wary of defining 'success' only in terms of keeping young people out of the system: there are other systems within our communities, which are equallly oppressive and dangerous; 'belief' systems which see violence, sexual oppression and racism as acceptable and normal.

A social approach

Our research has led us to conclude that the various youth services, allied with the education services, provide the most natural vehicle for evolving an intervention strategy; and these should represent the key site around which the intervention by other agencies should cluster. Schools, as they are the agency which works routinely with the broadest cross-section of young people, occupy an important position and are a valuable point of entry for intervention. Some of the projects funded under the DES Educational Support Grant (ESG) initiative of 1986, visited as part of our research on social crime prevention, have provided useful illustrations of the broad range of work that can be carried out through the school structure, from general crime awareness work through to sophisticated work with groups of children, or using the curriculum as a means of making young people aware of relevant issues in their environment. The school itself is also a site of tension, often a kind that has spilled over from the community, and work within schools can ease tension of this kind. We are concerned not only with the vulnerability of schools to various crimes such as vandalism, but also with the school as a key site where antisocial attitudes centring on crime, violence, racism and sexism, which originate in the community, are actively reproduced in a setting which all too frequently heightens rather than lowers these tensions. We have become aware, during the course of research visits, of the ways in which the school can become a surrogate focus for conflicts within the wider community and how these tensions can be refracted through the school to disastrous effects.

In Liverpool, for example, a school was established at the beginning of the 1980s, which was an amalgamation of a number of schools rigidly demarcated by religion and race. Putting them together created violent conflict; the school was picketed by some white parents and the National Front, and this led to counter-pickets by black separatist groups. There were running battles in the corridors, teachers were attacked, heroin was sold openly and – at one stage – a network of child prostitution attached itself to the school. The school was dubbed a 'race hate school' by the national media, and it was impossible to recruit women to work in the canteen because it became a battleground every lunch-time. The school now has changed almost out of recognition as the result of work done by the staff in conjunction with a local project run by a particularly charismatic figure. This man runs the Liverpool 8 Garden Farm and an organisation known as the 'Diggers' which undertakes environmental work in Liverpool. Links between the school and this organisation have evolved in such a way that the scheme has actually become an integral part of the school curriculum, offering art and environmentally based studies. The school boasts a very successful angling club (which is offered in the curriculum), and recently the scheme received £1,000 from the BBC Children in Need Appeal. The Diggers helped by bringing older people into the school, particularly during lunch breaks, which calmed the atmosphere, and they set up a project within the school intended to provide a focus for shared work. At the centre of the school – the very site of previous conflicts – there now stands an ornamental Japanese Garden.

To some extent these conflicts need to be traced back to their origins within the wider community; work in the school has to be actively linked to work within the community setting. The various youth and community services can play a valuable role in the process. Under the ESG initiatives this process has been encouraged; a scheme in Wolverhampton in particular attempts to integrate the school and the community setting. Similarly a scheme in Bradford has attempted to use the school structure as a means of resolving racial difficulties which arise as a result of the separation of races within the wider community. Not all schemes, though, have been as successful in recruiting the enthusiasm of the youth services. Branches of the youth services which deal with sport and leisure have been particularly slow in changing their focus; they still tend to have a very institutionalised approach, centring their work on youth clubs which are often quite rigidly policed, very quickly turning away, or turning off, the very young people who need them most. This is unfortunate because some of the best work we have seen in our research has been undertaken by innovative youth workers who have attempted to cater for those young people who most often feel excluded from mainstream youth activity. These schemes – funded increasingly by grants from bodies such as the IT Fund – focus on cultural and recreational work (not just activities like sport which tend to favour young people aleady successfully integrated into school).

Imaginative work in girls' groups and in groups for ethnic minorities has provided interesting insights here. It is clear that mainstream youth and recreational activities tend to reward young people who are already winners and who perhaps need them least. Other groups may find them irrelevant; certainly the groups of young people interviewed at the CAVE project (Community and Vocational Education) in Lambeth said they never used youth clubs, reflecting the views of the group in Midtown where it was found that most young people who had been in trouble with the police felt unwanted by the youth clubs. The need for a more flexible attitude and a process of de-institutionalisation has been called for from a number of directions (Smith, 1987; Paley *et al*, 1986; John, 1986). The fact is, to adapt a line from Adrian Mitchell, that most young people ignore youth clubs because most youth clubs ignore most young people. This problem surfaces clearly in crime prevention work (it has always been present for social workers, IT workers, probation officers and police officers attempting to reintegrate young people into their communities) because youth clubs run by sport and recreational divisions of local councils are reluctant to become involved. On a visit to a new juvenile-centred social crime prevention project in Salford the researcher was told that the Sport and Recreation division was so hostile that they had been effectively by-passed; inter-agency work was carried out with all the other relevant agencies, and it was hoped that eventually this one unhelpful agency could be presented with a *fait accompli*, but only after the project had been seen to be successful.

The CAVE (Community and Vocational Education) scheme is in many respects a typical example of well-established practice in Lambeth, which was the site of many of the earliest voluntary charitable initiatives in child care and has maintained a traditional of integrating professional and voluntary services. In keeping with this tradition the CAVE project has a core of professional school teachers to provide continuity and professional expertise but has also managed to attract a group of some 40–50 local volunteers to provide literacy training. The project would deny that it was involved in social crime prevention in a direct sense but recognises that the prevention of crime could be a positive, if not always an intended, consequence of work with young people who had 'given up' on school and were embarking on criminal careers largely as a result of truancy.

The CAVE Project runs three schemes, a Truancy Unit for young people of school age who are persistent truants, a Literacy Unit which caters for 14–25-year-olds and the Educational and Employment project catering for the 16–19-year-old age group. The young people in the Truancy Unit, who are referred by professionals or just, on occasion, refer themselves, explained that they used to spend their time wandering in the West End, frequently shop-lifting and becoming involved in other crimes. The project provides a supportive and stimulative environment for these young people, frequently giving them the close relationships that are difficult to maintain in a large impersonal school. The attendance rate in the units is consistently extremely high. The Literacy Unit also has referrals from professionals, but the majority of users, some 60%, are beyond school age and just refer themselves. The unit runs literacy programmes and cultural activities such as drama and art. The project is beginning to find that many of the young people who use the scheme are coming back as volunteers themselves; there are more young, unemployed and black volunteers and fewer 'young professionals' than there used to be. The Educational and Employment project has a strong vocational theme and provides literacy and numeracy skills to young people who, for whatever reason, failed to achieve at school. The co-ordinator explained that local black people in particular (and especially the girls) were anxious to achieve and felt that school had offered little to them.

One intriguing and very revealing aspect of this project is the referral and self-referral patterns when broken down by race. Those referred by professionals to the Truancy Unit were all white and so were the majority referred to the Literacy Unit; however, the majority of those who volunteered for the literacy and educational units were black, 60 % and 70 % respectively. We do not know why so few young black people were referred, when many of the older ones confessed to having been persistent truants, but suggest that such an obvious discrepancy in referral patterns demonstrates a need to develop new ways of working in schools and communities that are sensitive to the needs of black children, especially since the high use of the unit by older black youths and young adults ridicules the supposition that black people lack motivation.

The Birmingham Social Crime Prevention Unit represents quite a radical departure in Britain, as it is the first such scheme seeking to develop a social crime prevention approach. The starting point for the project was the Home Office Circular 8/84 which called for greater awareness of the need to prevent crime. The underlying philosophy was one of developing a broader response than could be provided by any one of the isolated agencies. The scheme is based in the west of Birmingham which has a very wide racial mix and includes places such as Handsworth as well as the city centre; therefore it has to consider crime problems within multi-racial communities as well as those forms of crime specific to new purpose-built shopping malls such as the Bull Ring. The scheme has had, therefore, to develop a broad strategy for its work, encompassing long-term work not only with young people but with the agencies and private institutions with whom young people come into contact in their daily lives. The workers see a need to approach the problem of young people and crime on three interrelated levels: firstly at the level of the young people and their cultures, secondly at the level of the community, and thirdly at the level of the statutory agencies who socialise young people. The Birmingham team believes that dealing with young people in isolation is inadeaquate, and that, rather, work must also be done with the formal and informal systems within which young people gain their social identities. This is becoming a discernible strand in current thinking in the social crime prevention field: a belief that the wider community must be educated to take a more tolerant attitude toward young people and recognise its responsibility toward them. This may take the form of local communities becoming more involved in the lives of its youth, local media not stereotyping young people and sensationalising their behaviour, shops and businesses taking a responsible stance by not displaying goods in places where the young will be tempted to take them, and statutory agencies not labelling and stigmatising young people with whom they come into contact.

The project workers set out their aims and philosophy thus:

> Social Crime Prevention is defined as any positive collective action which is intended to ameliorate through the process of education, crime awareness and the influencing of policies, any social factors that may induce or encourage criminal behaviour. Thus improving the condition of life in Society.

This broad definition recognises the need for a collective solution to the problem of crime rather than isolated piecemeal solutions. Thus far the scheme is very much in its infancy and its strategy requires a long-term approach.

The wide range of schemes funded under the Educational Support Grant initiative of 1986 provides an important focus for crime prevention work. As they are situated within schools and involve, in the main, a significant input by the Youth and Community services they may represent a means of working in a non-individualised, non-labelling way with a broad range of young people in a natural setting, thus overcoming some of the labelling problems which often follow as a consequence of intervention by other statutory agencies such as the police and social services. The schemes vary considerably in their primary orientation. Some are principally involved with the problems of racism in schools and the community, others with the problem of social dissaffection, others with vandalism. All are concerned to develop a multi-agency aspect of their work and wish to involve the wider community. The Sheffield ESG, for example, has its origins in a Crime Prevention Working group which was a multi-agency forum guided by NACRO, and the scheme has a commitment to involve the local community in its work. As an illustration of the potential for diversity we shall briefly describe the Thameside ESG because of its unusual focus.

This project has developed on links made between the Education and Youth Service in Thameside and an organisation called Community Pride, a voluntary movement aiming to improve the quality of the environment via the mobilisation of young people in the community. The director of the project believes that the school should be at the centre of any scheme designed to improve the environment and that a respect for the environment is a necessary component of any

Social Education approach. As in many of the schemes we have contacted, the staff believe that merely 'target hardening' in schools only 'raises the stakes and increases the challenge'; therefore young people need to be given opportunities to become involved with and learn to respect their environment. This is a philosophy which underpins the work of other environmentally based projects, which have had success in lowering vandalism rates in schools, such as the Diggers in Liverpool mentioned above.

Current practice in Scotland provides a useful counterpoint to these developments in England. This is valuable because in Scotland Intermediate Treatment never became, to such an extent as in England and Wales, a separate specialism reserved for recognised offenders and situated outside the youth service. This is obviously connected with the existence in Scotland of a very different system of juvenile justice, and the related phenomena of a lower level of incarceration of juveniles and a higher level of incarceration of young adults, for whom, in the absence of a probation service, services appear to be very underdeveloped. The Director of the IT Resource centre in Glasgow considers that social crime prevention should encapsulate the best elements of the work of NACRO's Safe Neighbourhoods Unit in combination with the emphasis on community development of the 'social action' approach advocated by those in IT critical of the 'new orthodoxy'. The IT Resource Centre has initiated work on a safe neighbourhood unit in Strathclyde with four workers. Generally, however, the police in Scotland are unwilling to be involved in joint work on crime prevention; Strathclyde is more advanced in this regard than other areas. It has what it calls a 'corporate strategy' which involves links between housing and other agencies under the safe neighbourhood initiative.

There is a wide variety of projects operating a 'social action' rather than a crime prevention model. IT is involved in many as it still works on a wide range of activities including outreach and detached youth work. Some are separately funded by the social work or community education departments, and tend to have a policital commitment to youth enfranchisement, which is reflected in Strathclyde's official policy documents. For example, in the statement 'Working with Young People' there is a criticism of traditional youth work.

> There is a danger that both community education workers and social workers will be trapped into ineffectual crisis responses to 'problem youth' rather than working long and hard with the local community to build up a framework of opportunities for young people which, at the very least, will act preventively to stop some problems arising (Strathclyde Regional Council, 1987).

Many of these projects are funded by Urban Aid; Strathclyde receives 80 % of Scotland's allocation. There are reservations about how successful this proliferation of projects has been: resources dry up, there tends to be little continuity of staffing, many schemes end up as coffee shops rather than as enabling agencies. In Edinburgh (Lothian Region), initiatives tend to be in the voluntary sector, with local authority funding which is long-term to the extent that projects have the support of local politicians. Again, the stated radicalism of the local council is reflected in the aims of local projects, which are usually described as 'urban survival strategies' rather than as being specifically concerned with crime prevention.

In this chapter we have outlined some of the contemporary issues in youth social work. The problems of racism and sexism compound the very real problems all working-class young people face in modern Britain, in which they are becoming increasingly marginalized. A social approach to youth-related problems does not seek to separate crime from the other problems that young people face: indeed over-emphasising crime at the expense of other difficulties can serve to intensify the marginalisation process. A social approach can also recognise the extent to which young people are themselves 'victims', not just of crime, but of a range of economic and social policies which inevitably lead to their loss of citizenship. The social crime prevention approach poses a challenge to all the agencies who become involved with young people, to deal with them less as individual 'cases' to be managed within the boundaries of their own 'system' and more as real social beings, struggling for survival in an increasingly hostile and unsympathetic society.

4 Prisons and sentencing trends

'Today, we face a crisis in Britain's prisons,' announces the back cover of a recent Penguin Special by the Director of NACRO (Stern, 1987). Nobody, including many members of the prison service itself, is likely to dispute that statement. What is particularly depressing about it is that it could have been said with equal truth at any time in the last twenty years. Indeed, according to Michel Foucault (1977), it would have been true for the last 150 years or so, ever since the establishment of something like our present system of imprisonment in the first decades of the nineteenth century. Foucault argues that as soon as the 'penitentiary' was invented, its failures were recognised; and there is certainly evidence of continuing (and, sadly, recurring) problems in implementing the ideals of the prison reformers of the late eighteenth century. It is doubtlessly the case that some problems are inherent and inevitable in any prison system, based on such questions as: how much freedom should prisoners be allowed? How should they be categorised? How can prison avoid increasing their problems and the likelihood of their re-offending? And (the question asked by the Roman poet Juvenal), who will guard the guards? While such problems form the core set of reasons for the opposition to the prison system, and for trying to find other ways of dealing with offenders, they are not what mainly concern us here. The British prison system has problems in common with those of other countries, but it also has problems that are distinctively its own.

Numbers

For one thing, Britain consistently has a higher proportion of its population behind bars than almost any other western European country. The Council of Europe produces a twice-yearly 'Prison Information Bulletin' covering its member countries. For February

1987, the Bulletin showed that in the Netherlands 37 people were in prison out of every 100,000 inhabitants; there were 50 in Norway, 57 in Italy and Sweden, 67 in Spain, 84 in West Germany and 89 in France. The figure for the United Kingdom as a whole was 96, exceeded only by Luxembourg, Turkey and Austria. However, the overall UK figure conceals discrepancies: the England and Wales figure was 94, the figure for Scotland was 109, and that for Northern Ireland was 121. Both Scottish and Northern Irish figues are substantially higher than the next highest, 103 in Austria. The figure for Northern Ireland no doubt arises mainly from the political situation there, but this cannot explain the Scottish figure, or indeed why the figure for England and Wales is so high, when a great deal of political and legislative effort over the past twenty years has gone into reducing it.

Another peculiarity, and a depressing one, of the British prison system is that compared with other countries its prison population contains a high proportion of young people. Of the prison population in September 1987 over 25 % were under 21, a figure surpassed only by Ireland, and almost double the proportion in France. Since, as we shall see, the number of juveniles in prison department custody has declined sharply during the 1980s, the figure means that this country is particularly inclined to imprison its young adults – a fact rather belatedly acknowledged in its penal policy. While this chapter is concerned with issues in the formal criminal justice system, it should be remembered, too, that there are forms of custody other than those managed by the prison service, including those which Stewart and Tutt (1987) describe as 'hidden'. They found that it was impossible to discover exactly how many juveniles were held on a given day in what were in effect custodial conditions, although they might be dignified with the name of treatment, in child care institutions and in hospitals.

The 1987 Council of Europe data also show changes in the proportion of the population in prison since 1983. Most countries show an increase, a substantial one for France (31 %) and Scotland (9 %). But other countries and jurisdictions show a decrease, including West Germany (18 %) and Italy (11 %); and there has been a 25 % decrease in Northern Ireland. There is, it seems, no universal law that decrees that prison populations must rise. Feest (1988) has outlined some reasons for the decrease in West Germany. He suggests that the explanation lies within the criminal justice system rather than in wider social changes. There has been a reduction in remands in custody, countering the 'well known psychological tendency on the part of judges to make the prison term fit (at least) the time already spent on remand' (p 3); and there has been a reduction in prosecutions, and an increased use of measures similar to cautions, along with reparation and informally imposed fines. According to Feest, various community-based projects have also exercised an influence, providing accommodation or work for people who would otherwise have been remanded in custody, and a wide range of 'alternatives', including victim–offender reconciliation, community work, training and supervised activities. Feest suggests that the 'alternatives movement', a 'criminal policy from below', has exercised its influence less by directly diverting offenders from prosecution or custody than by changing local public opinion and educating criminal justice officials, many of whom are directly involved in the projects.

It seems reasonable to start this chapter on a hopeful note, because there is quite widespread fatalism in Britain about the growth in the prison population, and doubt as to whether anything can halt it. It is useful, then, to be reminded that there is nothing inevitable about it; it has been reversed in a country similar in its relevant characteristics to Britain. There may well be, as Box (1987) suggests, a connection between the level of imprisonment and the level of unemployment, but the West German unemployment rate increased while the prison population fell. It seems more useful, as Rutherford (1984) has forcefully argued, to see a rising prison population as the product of a conscious policy choice ('choosing to expand', in Rutherford's phrase); or at any rate as the result of a refusal to consider other choices. The West German criminal justice system is of course not identical with the British (in any of its forms); but it is similar enough (especially since the creation of the Crown Prosecution Service) for it to be capable of providing useful lessons.

Cross-national comparisons are always likely to be problematic, but they also help to illuminate ways in which local problems might be tackled. One frequent source of confusion in the discussions of prison problems is a failure to distinguish between receptions into prison (the number of people who get locked up within a given period) and the prison population (the number of people who are locked up on a given date). Bottomley and Pease (1986) give a clear account of why it is important to make the distinction. Using 1983 statistics, they show that untried prisoners and convicted prisoners awaiting sentence (that is, prisoners on remand) together accounted for 41 % of receptions into prison, but for only 18 % of the average population; while sentenced prisoners accounted for 57 % of receptions, but for 82 % of the average population. The reason for the difference is that 'the prison population contains a higher proportion of long-sentence prisoners than does a cohort of receptions' (p 97). The prison population is a function of average sentence length as well as of the number of receptions.

Bottomley and Pease use this fact in two interesting ways. The first sheds further light on international comparisons on the use of imprisonment. The Council of Europe data for 1984 showed that the Netherlands and West Germany had similar rates of reception into prison (just over 200 per 100,000 inhabitants), but the West German prison population was about three times as high, in proportional terms, as the Dutch. The reason was that the average period of detention in West Germany was over six months, while in the Netherlands it was just over six weeks. By contrast, while Spain and Denmark had similar average populations, Denmark had a committal rate over twice as high as Spain's. The picture of prison use derived from the two kinds of statistics is very different (though England and Wales score highly – or badly – on both measures).

The second argument of Bottomley and Pease is that the long-established attempt to reduce the prison population by substituting non-custodial for custodial sentences is 'likely to provide a very low-geared means of reducing the prison population' (p 107). (This does not mean that it is not justified on other grounds – but if the aim is to bring the prison population down, there are better ways of proceeding.) 51 % of sentenced receptions in 1983 were of people given sentences of six months or less, but they accounted for only 17 % of the average population. This short-sentence group is presumably the group most likely to be considered for non-custodial measures, but what the figures mean is that in order to reduce the sentenced prison population by 17 % it would be necessary for the courts to be persuaded to impose non-custodial sentences in over half the cases where they now impose custodial ones. Similarly, to take a group often thought to be potentially 'divertible' from prison, fine defaulters accounted in 1983 for over 21,000 receptions into prison, but there were only 900 of them in the average population. Bottomley and Pease conclude, like other commentators (Rutherford, 1984), that a reduction in the prison population is more likely to be achieved by other means (for example, reducing the average length of sentences) than by encouraging the use of 'alternatives' to custody which may not be used as such at all (a point to be taken up later).

Feest's (1988) account suggests, however, that the development of non-custodial measures may contribute to a reduced prison population, if not by direct diversion, then by fostering a changed sentencing climate; and it is important to remember that the arguments for non-custodial measures do not depend for their validity on their effectiveness in reducing the prison population (there are many offenders who on grounds of humanity and justice should not be received into prison, however little their diversion would contribute to a reduction in the population). In the following chapters we look at some British evidence on the potential of alternatives, particularly in the juvenile system, to reduce the prison population. It is also worth noting that in the last few years there has been a considerable increase in the proportion of the prison population who are on remand, awaiting trial or sentence; the latest (1987) figures show that they accounted for 22 % of the total. Feest's analysis would suggest that they are a highly 'divertible' group, as would the fact that 39 % of men and 58 % of women remanded in custody do not end up with a prison sentence. There is evidence, too, that black people are more likely to be refused bail than whites (NACRO, 1986) – one of a number of signs of discrimination against black people in criminal justice (of which more later). Overall, there may be more scope for reducing the prison population by promoting the use of alternatives than Bottomley and Pease suggest – which is not to argue that this should be the main, still less the only way in which the problem is tackled.

About 96 % of the prison population in England and Wales are male (the figure is higher in Scotland and Northern Ireland). This has meant, among other things, that until recently the discussion of the prison system has concentrated entirely on male prisons. Following Carlen (1983), however, several studies have appeared which acknowledge the special problems women in prison face, partly as a result of their relatively small numbers. Because there are only seven exclusively female prisons in England and Wales, women are very likely to be imprisoned a long way from home, making it difficult for family and friends to visit. It is also clear from prison department reports that the rate of prescription of mood-changing drugs is consistently higher in women's than in men's prisons: Bottomley and Pease (1986) comment that 'while for the system as a whole an average of 28 doses of psychotropic or hypnotic drugs were administered, in women's prisons the average inmate receives a staggering 195 doses per year' (p 111). The difference between men and women in prison in this respect is hard to explain, but if one takes the dimmest view the figures suggest a high use of medication as a means of control (the so-called 'liquid cosh') in women's prisons, and on any view the level of use of these drugs suggests that many women in prison are very unhappy indeed.

The best-known indicator that there is a crisis in the prison system is overcrowding, but, as will become clear, this problem is far from universal. The prison service report for England and Wales for 1987–88 (Prison Service, 1988) records that the population at the end of March 1988 was 50,500, which included 1,300 in police cells. This represented a decline from a peak in the previous July of 51,200: seasonal fluctuations are normal, and are proverbially, and perhaps really, associated with judges' holidays. The 'certified normal accommodation' of the system was 43,690, so the overall extent of overcrowding can easily be calculated. At the population peak in July 1987, 5,091 prisoners were 'three'd up' – three in a cell designed for one – and a further 13,892 were sharing a cell with one other man. The report comments on the steep rise in the population since 1985, noting that the main growth has been in the number serving longer sentences (four years and over for men, three years and over for women). The number of unsentenced prisoners had risen by 4 % (a long-term trend), while the number of young offenders (under 21) had decreased by 5 %.

One important feature of the prison population is that it contains a considerably higher proportion of people from ethnic minority groups than the population as a whole. According to Home Office figures published in 1986 (cf. Crow, 1987), around 12 % of male prisoners belonged to minority ethnic groups, about twice the figure which would be expected from their representation in the total population, and the disporportion was even higher for women prisoners. Within this total, people of Afro-Caribbean origin were particularly over-represented, while there were if anything fewer people with origins in the Indian subcontinent than would have been expected. The disproportion was greater for remanded than for sentenced prisoners, and black prisoners tended to have fewer previous convictions than whites sentenced for comparable offences.

There are evident grounds here for thinking that there is discrimination against black people in the criminal justice system, which could operate at any one, or all, of the various stages of decision-making. It is not necessarily the case (although we examine the evidence in more detail later) that courts regularly sentence in a racist manner; the crucial decisions could have been taken at an earlier stage. For example, Crow (1987) cites an unpublished paper by Ken Pease, based on British Crime Survey data, which suggests that the perceived ethnic origin of the offender affects the likelihood that the victim will report the crime to the police. Since no processing by the criminal justice system can take place if a crime is not reported, this means that 'the first stage in making offenders available to the penal system is discriminatory' (p 305). It is also likely that a higher proportion of black than of white offenders are detected by the police: both Smith and Gray (1983) and Willis (1985) concluded that black people, especially young Afro-Caribbean males, were much more likely than whites to be stopped and searched by the police (though without a generally higher 'strike rate'). Another possibility, suggested by Landau and Nathan (1983), is that young black offenders are more likely than their white counterparts to be prosecuted and less likely to be cautioned. While the process may not be wholly clear, the outcome is: black people are disproportionately likely to suffer the ultimate penalty the law permits, and in prison they are likely to experience further racist discrimination, at least if one is to judge by prison officers' published comments (Stern, 1987, pp 99–10).

Returning to the question of overall numbers: the latest prison service report notes that the problems arising from overcrowding would have been a good deal worse had the population not been cut, at a stroke, by 3,000 in August 1987. This was achieved by the device of introducing half-sentence remission (instead of one-third) for all prisoners serving sentences of twelve months or less. That is, prisoners sentenced to twelve months, for example, who would have expected actually to serve eight months, found that they were eligible for release after six. This was the latest of several efforts by the executive to reduce the prison population by introducing devices for early release. The best-known of these devices is parole, which was extended by the 1982 Act to cover, in effect, all prisoners serving sentences of ten-and-a-half months or more (the previous minimum sentence had been eighteen months). Remission of sentences is also clearly a means by which the executive can alter the length of a sentence imposed by the court.

Not all these executive interventions work in the same direction. For instance, Leon Brittan, the then Home Secretary, told the Conservative Party Conference in 1983, at the same time as he announced the reduction of the minimum eligibility period for parole, that nobody sentenced to more than five years for violence would get parole at all, unless there were 'genuinely exceptional' circumstances. This is an unusually clear example of the phenomenon of 'bifurcation', first noted by Bottoms (1977): the tendency for the system to get 'softer' at the bottom end and 'harder' at the top. The annual Parole Board Reports since then show that very few of the prisoners in this restricted category are paroled for more than a few weeks, so it is clear that the circumstances have to be very exceptional indeed. The point we want to make is that the various well-established ways in which the executive can interfere with judicial sentences suggest that there is nothing sacrosanct about the supposed foundation of the British constitution, the separation of powers between the judiciary and the executive. From the point of view of the feasibility of such executive measures as Rutherford (1984) and others have suggested as a means of reducing the prison population, this is encouraging: there are plenty of precedents for the erosion of judicial independence. The process has gone so far already, often in an *ad hoc*, piecemeal fashion, that constitutional lawyers need not worry too much about further extensions of executive powers.

It is important to realise, however, that overcrowding was far from being a problem in every prison, even in 1988. In fact, it has for years been exclusively a problem of local prisons and remand centres for men. This means that unsentenced prisoners and those serving the shortest sentences generally have to endure the worst physical conditions the prison system has to offer. The most depressing and disgusting images of prison life – cell-sharing, slopping-out, twenty-three hours a day spent in a stinking cell – derive from the local prison experience. In Armley prison in Leeds, for example, the average population in 1987–88 was 1,338, with a peak of 1,410; the official capacity of the prison was 642. The comparable figures for Oxford prison were 240, 266 and 127, showing that the problem can exist on a smaller scale. It is unlikely that there was any point during the year when Armley accommodated less than twice as many men as it can officially contain. On the other hand, there were prisons which were not overcrowded at all, even some which were under-occupied, in that the average population was lower than the official capacity. What explains this apparent irrationality in the system?

The prisons which were least crowded were also the most expensive. In the prison service report quoted above, the cost of keeping an adult prisoner in an open prison in 1987–88 was given as £184 per week; in a local prison it was £248; for women the cost was £385; and for a 'dispersal' prison it was £557. The dispersal prisons, eight in number, are top-security establishments in which the supposedly most dangerous men in the prison system, those in security category 'A', are dispersed. The alternative, advocated in 1966 in the Mountbatten Report which introduced the present security classification, would be to concentrate these men in a single maximum security establishment. This option was rejected, mainly because of anxieties about the control problems which such an undiluted concentration of dangerous men with little to lose would present, and the dispersal system came into being.

The obvious problem with it is that the majority of men housed in dispersal prisons by definition do not need the very high level of security to which they are subjected: only about 20 % of men in these prisons are in the top security category for which the prisons are designed. The system is thus 'driven' by the security requirements of the officially very dangerous, while the officially not so dangerous, whose presence is required as dilution, are placed in institutions which are often far from their home areas, and equipped with security and control facilities in excess of their needs. Another problem is that there is something fishy about the security classifications themselves. Nobody will deny that there are some men in prison for whom escape should be made as hard as human ingenuity can make it, but this does not mean that the classifications have a scientific basis. Stern (1987) quotes a lecture by Rod Morgan in which he showed that there is a very close relationship between the use of different security categories and the availability of different types of accommodation in each prison region. In the Midlands, for example, which had only 7 % of accommodation at category 'B' level, and 53 % at category 'C', 12 % of prisoners were categorised as 'B' – meaning that escape should be made very difficult although they were not in the most dangerous category – and 55 % as 'C'. In the South-East, which is more lavishly equipped with category 'B' prisons, with 22 % of accommodation at that level, 25 % of prisoners were duly classified as 'B'. The strong presumption must be that prisoners are categorised to suit the available accommodation. It is difficult to see how it could be otherwise, unless there were to be a guaranteed surplus of accommodation for each security category (which nobody advocates). Morgan argued that if every region categorised on the same basis as the Midlands, millions of pounds could be saved by avoiding the placement of prisoners in institutions which provide more security than is needed to prevent their escape.

We have seen, then, that the crisis in the prison system is only partly a crisis of numbers. Indeed, in the Scottish prison system overcrowding is not a major problem overall, with an excess of accommodation over population (Stern, 1987), and yet it has generated some of the most serious causes for concern, with violent disturbances at Peterhead and a spate of suicides in the young offenders' institutions at Glenochil (Scraton, Sim and Skidmore, 1988). Some at least of the problems in England and Wales could arguably be resolved by a more rational use of the resources the system has available at present; at the very least, some of the worst overcrowding could be alleviated. But the crisis has other dimensions, and we now want to examine these.

Control, legitimacy and morale

Fitzgerald and Sim (1982) suggest that the crisis in British prisons has five elements: visibility, authority, conditions, containment and legitimacy. We have discussed conditions, and want to concentrate here on the elements of authority, containment and legitimacy, although in a slightly altered form. By the crisis of visibility Fitzgerald and Sim meant that the traditional secrecy which envelops prison life was becoming harder to maintain, largely as a result of the efforts of prisoners' organisations. Since they wrote the process has been taken further, notably by the establishment in 1980 of an independent inspectorate, which publishes often critical reports on individual prisons and an annual review. The prison service has also (perhaps bowing to the inevitable) granted access to the media, for example in the series of television films about Strangeways prison in Manchester, with results that have been potentially damaging, at least to the trained eye. This is not too say that the prison service is not still inclined to keep its secrets whenever possible, and there is little doubt that many of its staff are unhappy about the new element of *glasnost*; but it is clear that there has been some change since Fitzgerald and Sim first wrote, at the end of the 1970s.

The dispersal prisons in England are exempt from problems of overcrowding (because this would pose evident problems of control), but they are the prisons in which the most serious disturbances have occurred. There have been what the Home Office calls 'major' disturbances in all but one of the long-established dispersal prisons; in one, Hull, the disturbance (in 1976) was serious enough to render it uninhabitable, and it has never rejoined the dispersal system. The dispersal prisons have proved successful in security terms – the helicopter esape from Gartree in 1987 was the first – but much less so in terms of internal control. Nor are problems of this kind confined to the prisons which house the longest-term prisoners: in 1988 there was a serious disturbance at Haverigg prison in Cumbria, supposedly because prisoners objected to the removal of pin-ups from their dormitory walls. Thomas and Pooley (1980) argue that prisoners are most likely to revolt when the authorities attempt to enforce rules strictly after a period in which they have been only loosely enforced; this certainly seems to have been the case at Hull. Whatever the reasons, there is nothing more embarrassing to the prison service than for the TV news to feature a film of prisoners on the roof; apart from the very real physical danger which a prison riot entails, for prisoners as well as officers, it is a sign that prisons are failing in one of their main tasks, the 'humane containment' of their inmates.

Another source of embarrassment arises from the behaviour not of prisoners but of their guards. The past two decades, and particularly the last ten years, have produced unparalleled evidence of the discontent and dissatisfaction many prison officers apparently feel. Most recently, there was the unique spectacle of Wandsworth prison being run by police officers because the prison officers had been locked out for refusing to accept new working arrangements. There are several reasons for the recurring industrial relations problems, and we can only give a quick sketch of them here. The most immediate (and the source of the trouble at Wandsworth) is the Home Office's attempt to introduce a new form of work organisation known as 'Fresh Start'. In the view of prison officers, the main motive behind Fresh Start is a wish to reduce the amount of overtime available to them, and there is no doubt that this does figure prominently in Home Office thinking. There are other elements in the plan which are intended to improve career opportunities, morale and commitment, but the prison officers' scepticism is understandable since these improvements would mean, for many of them, a cut in take-home pay (though an increase in the basic wage).

The implementation of Fresh Start, proposals for which first appeared in mid-1986, has been slow and painful in many prisons, and, one may guess, not helped by the Home Office's evident antagonism towards the Prison Officers' Association. Official suspicion and dislike of the working practices the POA has developed are among the reasons for the government's enthusiasm for involving the private sector in building and running prisons. In early 1989 Douglas Hurd, the Home Secretary, announced that private businesses would be invited to tender for contracts to build and run new remand centres. It is fair to say that when the idea of private prisons was first mooted in a paper from the Adam Smith Institute in 1984 it was treated by many commentators on penal policy as a bit of a joke. It became less funny with the publication in 1987 of a Select Committee report which favoured the involvement of private enterprise in the remand part of the system, and of a subsequent Green Paper in 1988. Major construction companies clearly believe that there is money to be made, in conjunction with various specially formed consortia, from running prisons on contract from the Home Office. It is tempting to wonder if judges and magistrates will rush to buy shares in these ventures, and what the effect on the prison population is likely to be. This is a striking instance of the Government's commitment to privatisation where at all possible, but the Home Secretary also made it clear that one of the attractions of the idea was that it would enable a truly 'fresh start' to be made, without the POA.

There are more deep-seated and chronic reasons for low morale in the prison service. The crisis of 'legitimacy' refers to the growing criticism of the entire prison system which can be traced at least to the mid-1960s, and which called into question the validity of the established claim that prison could have a reforming or rehabilitative effect on its inmates. We deal in the next chapter with some of the research evidence which challenged this claim; what is important here is the effect on prison service morale. In the early 1960s there was quite widespread optimism about the capacity of prisons not just to contain but to treat. Trasler (1962), writing from a psychological perspective, looked forward to a time in the near future, when prisons would be run on scientific psychological principles, and thus provide effective correctional treatment. This optimism was short-lived. The spectacular escapes of the spy George Blake and the train robber Ronald Biggs, which led to the setting up of the Mountbatten Committee on escapes and security, were widely interpreted as indicating that the reforming enthusiasm in the prison service had gone altogether too far, and that it was time to return to the traditional values of security and control. The aim of helping prisoners to lead 'a good and useful life' on release was tacitly abandoned in favour of the less ambitious goal of 'humane containment'. Members of the prison service increasingly accepted the critical view that prison was almost bound to make things worse for prisoners rather than better; prisons were to become human (and, it was hoped, humane) warehouses. The result has been the 'moral vacuum' identified by the May Report (Home Office, 1979), which, the Committee feared, would lead to the 'routine brutalization of all the participants'.

The trouble is that if the aim is officially defined merely as containment or storage it is harder to retain a commitment to doing this humanely than if you are allowed to take a more elevated view of the purpose of your work. This problem was identified by Thomas (1972), who sugested that the main reason for demoralisation among prison officers was that they had been gradually stripped of all functions apart from 'locking them up and counting them'. The potentially more satisfying jobs – education, welfare, treatment, preparing for release, and so on – had all been taken over by outside 'experts' (teachers, psychologists, probation officers, and so on) who enjoyed an undeservedly higher status than the poor 'screws'. The POA has tried to resist this erosion of the prison officer's job (as they see it); for example, they have consistently opposed the presence of probation officers in prison, and have argued that welfare and social work tasks should be undertaken by prison officers. (The view that probation officers should withdraw from prisons is shared, in a perhaps surprising convergence, by the probation officers' union, NAPO.)

While there is no doubt that its main aim is to increase effective management control in prisons, the Fresh Start programme tries in various ways to respond to the prison officers' dissatisfaction. One element is the introduction of a new structure which should make it easier for prison officers to rise through the ranks to the governing grades. Hitherto, it has been possible for entrants to the prison service with the right qualities of education, leadership and so on to enter the governing grades directly; from now on – bringing the prison service into line with the police and fire service – all new recruits will have to spend some time as prison officers, though some may be chosen for a 'fast track', an accelerated promotion scheme. Fresh Start also contains measures intended to improve the officers' job satisfaction and to foster positive motivation. For instance, it encourages the establishment of working groups of officers who would have regular responsibility for a particular group of inmates, and it is hoped that this will reduce the problems of discontinuity and inconsistency which arise when officers are liable to be posted, within a single day, from the wing to the gate lodge and back to another wing. Clearly such a system (if it can be called that) means that it is impossible for an officer to get to know any group of prisoners well, still less to begin to concern himself with their needs.

Fresh Start also encourages officers to become more involved in 'shared working' with probation staff on social work and welfare problems. Schemes of this sort have existed in some prisons, off and on, for many years, as part of an effort to increase job satisfaction among prison staff and improve working relations with probation officers. Jepson and Elliot (1986) surveyed and described these schemes, noting variations between prisons in the extent to which prison officers had become effectively involved in social work tasks. Although shared working is now supposed to be the norm, we are aware of continuing differences between prisons, which stem from varying levels of prison officer commitment and of overall staffing resources. It seems that shared working is likely to be quickly abandoned if other tasks demand the presence of prison officers: control and discipline, perhaps inevitably, take precedence over helping prisoners. Nevertheless some ambitious schemes are presently being tried, which aim to involve prison officers in such important work as discussing parole with prisoners and writing reports to the parole board; it remains to be seen whether they succeed in raising morale and, surely as important, improving the quality of the welfare of prisoners.

One possible outcome of such success would be that the role of probation officers in prison would shrink to the point of invisibility. Stewart and Smith (1987), commenting on the available evidence on the help given to juveniles in custody, suggest that there are grounds for concern about what would happen if probation officers withdrew entirely from prison work, and note that this concern is shared within the ranks of prison officers. Probation staffing in most institutions which house juveniles is already minimal (often just one senior probation officer with liaison functions), and Stewart and Smith found indications that this meant, paradoxically, that juveniles in prison were likely to have less access to help and advice than adults. There must be some doubt as to whether the prison service is ready and able (not to mention willing) to adopt the general helping role which probation officers, in principle at least, have carried out in prisons. If these doubts are well founded, so is the worry expressed by many probation officers that the NAPO policy of withdrawal from prisons will be implemented by stealth, in a gradual process of erosion of probation tasks.

We do not mean to suggest that it is wrong to try to improve morale in the prison service; it might be better if the effort to do this was not undermined by other aspects of government policy, including privatisation. People are more likely to try to do their job well if they feel that it is purposeful and valued, and a prison regime which is viewed simply as a means of storing people is less likely to achieve even this humanely than one which aims to provide an environment which, despite the inevitable impoverishment, is based on a determined effort to ensure that inmates' time is spent as constructively as possible. Otherwise we are left with the moral vacuum – and a prison system which could almost have been designed to increase the criminal potential of its inhabitants.

'Alternatives' to custody

The Government's established response (this applies to more than one government) to the crisis in prisons, especially the crisis of numbers, has been to introduce more measures which courts might use instead of custodial sentences, and to back up the legislation with encouraging noises to the effect that many offenders can be dealt with by community rather than custodial options. This policy, we have suggested, has not been notably successful, judging by the rise in the prison population and the trends over the past ten years in the use of various sentences. It is possible, of course, that things would have been worse without the introduction of new measures; but it is also possible that the new measures have themselves made things worse. For instance, the 1982 Criminal Justice Act introduced the option of partly suspending a prison sentence, and insofar as this measure is used when previously the sentence would have been wholly suspended rather than when none of it would have been suspended it will amount to direct diversion into, not away from, custody. This illustrates the general problem: how to ensure that the intended alteratives to custody are used as such, and not as alternatives to something else. A crude survey of changes in the use of different sentences does not in itself answer the question of what the alternatives are alternatives to, but it does provide a broad indication of what has been going on in criminal justice.

The latest criminal statistics (Home Office, 1988a) show changes in the use of various sentences over the period 1977–87. (All figures refer to indictable offences only, and sentences rather than persons are counted.) Taking the youngest age group first, the figures show a remarkable drop in the number of 10–13-year-olds sentenced, from 21,600 in 1977 to 4,600 ten years later. The number of girls has dropped proportionately more than the number of boys, from 2,400 to 300. The main reason, discussed in more detail later, is probably the increased use of cautions in this period. The pattern of sentencing shows an increase in the use of absolute and conditional discharges, given to 42 % of sentenced boys and 63 % of girls, and a decline in the use of all measures, including supervision and care, except for attendance centres, the use of which has increased from 14 % to 21 % for boys. But this still represents a reduction in the number of orders made from 2,600 to 900. We can say, then, that over these ten years the reaction of the criminal justice system to children who commit offences has become less interventionist. The figures cannot tell us whether there has been an increase in other forms of intervention, and there is evidence (e.g. Webb, 1984) that, other things being equal, girls are more likely than boys to be subjected to some form of welfare intervention, often on sexual grounds; but even if there has been an increase it is unlikely to invalidate the conclusion that these children are now dealt with – for their offending – in a less intrusive way than before.

The movements in the sentencing of 14–16-year-olds are in the same direction, but less dramatic. The total of those sentenced has declined from 78,100 to 37,300, with once more the larger proportional decline being among girls, from 7,500 to 3,100. The percentage of the use of discharges, attendance centre orders and community service has increased, while the use of supervision has increased for boys but not for girls, and there has been a decrease in the percentage of the use of fines and care orders (1 % of boys and 2 % of girls in 1987). The percentage of the use of immediate custody declined slightly for boys, from 12 to 11 %, but rose from 1 to 2 % for girls (representing a more or less constant number of 100 girls sentenced to custody in a year). Boys were much more likely to receive attendance centre orders, community service and custody than girls; gender differences in sentencing appear in all age groups, but it is difficult to make sense of them in the absence of information about differences in type and seriousness of offences committed by males and females, and in their histories of offending. If females appear to receive more lenient sentences, this is probably because by these measures they are less serious offenders (Farrington and Morris, 1983). On the other hand, some sentences (e.g. community service) seem to be regarded as particularly suitable for males, and others (e.g. probation) for females. This becomes clearer when we look at the figures for adults.

When we turn from juveniles to young adults we are at once dealing with much larger numbers, and the total of those sentenced has increased since 1977, though not steadily. In 1977 90,000 17–20-year-old males and 12,700 females received a court sentence; in 1982 the figures were 119,900 and 15,100; and in 1987 they had declined again to 99,900 and 12,200. In terms of sentencing trends, there has been a substantial decrease in the use of fines, though this is still the most widely used sentence (just under 40 % of all sentences). There has been a small increase in the use of discharges (up from 7 to 10 % for males and from 20 to 28 % for females) and of probation, which was at a historically low level in 1977 (up from 7 to 12 % for males and from 19 to 22 % for females). The use of community service has risen more sharply, from 6 to 13 % for males – but only from 2 to 5 % for females. The percentage of the use of immediate custody has increased from 18 to 21 % for males and from 3 to 5 % for females; a factor in this rise seems to have been the abolition in the 1982 Act of the option of suspending a prison sentence for young adults. The actual number receiving a custodial sentence was up from 16,400 in 1977, including 500 females, to 21,300 (600 females), but down from a peak of 25,300 in 1985.

Finally, the figures for sentencing of those aged 21 and over show, in general, some similar movements, but again it needs to be remembered that much larger total numbers are involved. The total for 1987 – 230,300 – was actually lower than for 1977, but this was entirely because fewer women were sentenced: the figure for women decreased from 45,000 (its highest in the ten-year period) to 32,000, that for men increased from 188,300 to 198,300 (following a peak of 216,000 in 1983). The use of fines for this group has decreased along lines similar to the decrease for young adults, while the discharges, probation, community service and custody has increased in percentage terms. Suspended sentences show an increase for women but a slight drop for men. Thus, comparing 1977 and 1987, the percentage figures for discharges were 8 and 10 % for men, 19 and 26 % for women, for probation 5 and 8 % for men, 12 and 18 % for women; for community service 2 and 7 % for men, 1 and 3 % for women; and for immediate custody 16 and 21 %, and 3 and 8 % respectively. In numerical terms, 42,000 men and 2,500 women received custodial sentences in 1987.

What sense can be made of these figures? Probably the most striking feature of the figures for all age groups, but especially for those aged 17 and over, is the decline in the use of fines. They are still the most often used sentence, but the percentage for their use has gone down from well around 55 % of all adult sentences to about 40 %. This might reasonably be associated with the rise in unemployment from the late 1970s; if unemployment rates decline, we might then expect to see a revival in the use of monetary penalties. What has happened to those offenders who would have been fined if the use of fines had remained at its 1977 level? The figures suggest that a few may have received discharges instead, but that rather some have been put on probation, given community service orders, or sent to prison. The use of probation and community service, widely canvassed as alternatives to custody, increased in these ten years, and so did the use of custody for adults. The rise in the use of non-custodial measures may then have been at the expense of another non-custodial measure, the fine, and not at the expense of custody.

From the sentencing figures themselves, this would necessarily be a tentative conclusion; but other evidence exists about the way in which these measures are used. Analysing the use of suspended sentences, the first major 'alternative to custody', Bottoms (1981) concluded that the new penalty was used no more than half the time in cases where there would previously have been an immediate prison sentence. One problem, according to Bottoms, may have been an ambiguity about the purpose of suspended sentences – and when community service was introduced, its purpose was similarly ambiguous. A suspended sentence could be justified as a deterrent, a sword of Damocles hanging over the offender's head and providing a useful reminder of the consequences of re-offending, and not on the grounds which the Government hoped sentencers would bear in mind, namely the desirability of reducing the prison population. Bottoms also found that when magistrates suspended a prison sentence the length of the sentence tended to be longer than in cases where they imposed an immediate sentence. In terms of the prison population, this is important becaues three out of ten people given a suspended sentence will be reconvicted during the period of suspension;

there is a strong likelihood (though not a legal requirement) that the suspended sentence will then be activated; and it is also likely that a prison sentence imposed for the new offence will be consecutive rather than concurrent. If all this happens, the offender will go to prison for longer than if an immediate prison sentence had been imposed for the original offence (and there is a 50 % chance that the suspended sentence was not imposed as an alternative to immediate custody anyway). As Bottomley and Pease (1986, p 91), to whom the foregoing discussion is indebted, comment: 'it is clear that any contribution made by the suspended sentence to the reduction of the prison population can only be marginal. More importantly, the operation is unfair.'

Although the mechanisms are different, it is equally unclear whether community service orders have contributed much to a reduction of the prison population. We discuss later the ambiguity which, perhaps deliberately, was allowed to surround their purpose when they were introduced in 1973, initially on an experimental basis. Their rapid growth over the next ten years is often regarded as an instance of successful innovation in penal policy (there are not many such), and they have been admired and imitated in other countries, including some, like the Netherlands, which we might have expected to know better. While it is still common to hear probation officers and others say that in their area at least community service is strictly used as an alternative to custody, the best estimates (Pease, 1985b) have consistently been that it is used in this way in only 45–50 % of all cases; so in 50–55 % of cases it is displacing another community option. It is inherently hard to measure this, but one way is an examination of what happens to those who breach the conditions of their orders and are brought back to court. You would expect the result to be a custodial sentence if this was what the original order was an alternative to, but in fact fewer than 40 % of those who breach the conditions of their orders receive custody – a similar percentage to that for breach of probation, which is usually thought to be below community service in the scale of seriousness of sentence.

We want now to discuss two issues which emerge less directly from the sentencing figures – the sentencing of women and of black people. The traditional view about the sentencing of women is that they are treated more leniently than men – the 'chivalry' hypothesis. This has recently been challenged by a number of writers, who have argued that the supposed leniency in the sentencing of women disappears when the seriousness of the offence and previous convictions are taken into account (Farrington and Morris, 1983; Eaton, 1986). Other writers have tried to set the sentencing of women within the context of stereotypical gender roles: for example, Dominelli (1984) connects the under-use of community service for women with dominant ideas about a woman's place being in the home. It is undoubtedly the case that while women may not receive less or more severe sentences than men convicted for similar offences and with similar criminal records, they do receive different sentences. This is particularly marked in the use of probation and community sevice. In 1987, under 6 % of adults who were sentenced to community service were women, compared with over 31 % of adults placed on probation. It seems that community service is thought of as a sentence for males, which means that women may in some areas at least face a shorter 'tariff' than men; the emphasis in recent Home Office statements on toughening up community service is likely to reinforce this tendency. On the other hand, it may be that probation is thought particularly appropriate for women because of a stereotypical view that a woman who commits an offence is more likely than a man to need help or treatment, offending being supposedly more alien to femininity than to masculinity.

Two final points may help to put into perspective the relative contributions of men and women to the criminal statistics, and their representation in the prison population. Farrington (1981) estimated the lifetime prevalence of convictions for men and women born in, say, 1960. His estimates are likely to seem startlingly high: 43 % of males and 14.7 % of females would, on his calculations, be convicted of an indictable offence at some time in their lives. Further research by the Home Office, using a different method of calculation, suggested that about 30 % of males born in 1953 had been convicted of an indictable offence by the age of 28, a finding broadly in line with Farrington's calculations (quoted in Harvey and Pease, 1988). Using a cross-sectional method like Farrington's, and basing their estimates on rates of first-time imprisonment in certain years, Harvey and Pease calculated the lifetime prevalence of imprisonment. Their lowest estimate for men was that one in twenty would at some time in his life be sentenced to custody, while the highest estimate for women was one in 160. The male figure here again seems startlingly high, but the discrepancy between the male and female conviction rates and the corresponding imprisonment rates cannot simply be taken as providing support for the chivalry hypothesis, since convicted men are likely to have committed more, and more serious, crimes than convicted women.

As suggested above, there is also evidence that black people are more at risk of imprisonment than whites. As we have seen, there are some grounds for thinking that this may be an outcome of decisions made at the early stages of the criminal justice process: by police officers who may discriminate between suspects on racial grounds; by the police and others who decide whether to recommend a prosecution or a caution; and even by victims, whose decision to report or not report an offence can be influenced by the perceived racial origin of the offender. A number of studies have also investigated sentencing practice, and related sentences to the social inquiry reports prepared for the courts by probation officers and social workers. The evidence is, as with the sentencing of females, ambiguous and sometimes contradictory; summaries can be found in Crow (1987) and Waters (1988). There seems to be no general evidence that courts impose harsher sentences on black (Afro-Caribbean or Asian) than on white defendants, but there is some evidence of difference. Pinder (1984), for instance, found that black women were more likely than any other group to be recommended for and receive probation, while black men were more likely than any other group to be recommended for and receive community service. They seemed to be the least likely group to be put on probation.

Another study by Mair (1986) noted further connections between the process of decision-making and its outcomes. He found that recommendations in reports were similar for all ethnic groups, but that the two magistrates' courts he studied were most inclined to ask for reports on Afro-Caribbean defendants, and least inclined to do this for Asians. Black defendants were less likely to be put on probation, but they were also less likely to be sentenced to immediate imprisonment; they were more likely to be given community service or a suspended sentence. A very different approach is taken by Walker (1987), who suggests that the assumption that the over-representation of Afro-Caribbeans in the prison population is evidence of racism somewhere in the system is unwarranted; she suggests that if age and social class are taken into account the proportion of Afro-Caribbeans in prison may be close to what one would expect, since a high proportion of this ethnic group is young and of lower social class, and therefore anyway more likely to offend and be arrested, so that the issues of race and racism may be irrelevant.

We think this is doubtful, and not simply on the grounds that you can do anything with statistics (especially if you understand them better than your readers). While the evidence on sentencing practice is not conclusive, there are good reasons for thinking that young black people, especially Afro-Caribbeans, are more likely to be drawn into the criminal justice system, and less likely to be diverted from it at an early stage, than their white counterparts. We think, too, that the approach represented by Pinder (1984), with its close attention to the nuances of language and tone in social inquiry reports, has had a strong and healthy influence on social work agencies, in making the workers aware of the ways in which racist messages can be covertly conveyed, whatever the intentions of the writers (for an account of hidden racism in social work, see Dominelli, 1988). There is still a great deal of work to be done, but we are encouraged by the signs we pick up from contact with practitioners that many agencies have become serious about actively developing an anti-racist practice. For example, some probation areas have set up panels which examine reports prepared on black defendants to ensure that racist language or imagery is not included, in however subtle a form. Action of this kind is likely, at least in the short term, to entail pain and conflict, but it is an example of what social work agencies can do to minimise their share in the imprisonment of black people (and, as we shall suggest in the following chapters, it is in line with the distinctive values which social work can bring to criminal justice).

The general tone of this chapter has inevitably been bleak. It is impossible to review the prison system and the attempts over the past twenty years to alleviate its chronic crisis without some feeling of gloom. Nevertheless, we hope to have suggested that the struggle to achieve a more rational, humane and constructive system is still worth pursuing. There are examples from elsewhere, especially in recent times from West Germany, to suggest that progressive change is possible, even in a country with a tradition of punitiveness in dealing with offenders. The change, we should remember, has come about largely through shifts in attitude within the criminal justice system, without more widespread social change: real reform and improvement are possible this side the revolution. It seems to us impossibly difficult and Utopian to argue that the prison system should be abolished; we agree that there are some people who should be locked up, for the protection of the rest of us. But it is perfectly possible to argue that the prison system should be much smaller and also that its mandate should be something more than the storage of unwanted people, and this is why we think that any efforts to restore a sense of value and purpose in the prison service should be supported – provided that this is accompanied by a commitment to reducing the overall size of the system. Rutherford (1984) has performed a valuable service in reminding us that the seemingly inevitable expansion of the system is actually not inevitable at all, but the result of a series of choices. That means that different choices are possible. Some of them will be about the place of social work within the criminal justice process; and it is with social work that the next two chapters are concerned.

5 Developments in social work (i): Research and adult offenders

The aim of this and the following chapter is to describe and discuss developments in social work with offenders over (roughly) the past twenty years, and to set these in the context of changes in penal policy and criminological thinking. The historical account is both factual and thematic: that is, we try to give a reasonably full account of significant events during this period, and to show how they illustrate the recurrence of certain themes and preoccupations. Towards the end of the next chapter we discuss at greater length some current arguments within social work about how work with offenders should develop; we have views on this like everyone else, and we shall make our preferences clear.

For the sake of clarity we discuss developments in the adult and juvenile sectors separately; this makes sense, since they are affected by different legislation, have different patterns of funding and organisation, are staffed by different departments and in some ways have different traditions and working practices. All the same, it is important to remember that many of the themes which have been important in work with adult offenders have also influenced policy and practice with juveniles, and *vice versa*; so to some extent the split is an artificial one, and our own compartments are far from watertight. Indeed, we shall argue that one of the most striking features about recent policy statements on social work with adult offenders is how much they are influenced by developments in work with juveniles. To many workers there may have been little obvious cross-fertilisation between the two sectors; but at other levels, perhaps reflecting what Cohen (1985) calls the 'master patterns' in deviancy control, their development has a good deal in common.

Research

This is clear, for example, if one considers the most influential
research in this period. The broad outlines of this research, as it was
understood in the context of criminological theory and penal policy,
have been traced in Chapter 1. Here we want to examine in more
detail the research that had a specific impact on social work. This
research, roughly speaking, is of two kinds: a first phase of research
on the outcomes of social work with offenders, and a second phase
which emphasised the importance of understanding the system in
which social workers and their clients are enmeshed. While there is
always room to question how far social workers attend to research
findings (and some people argue that they pay no attention at all!),
there seems little doubt that the first phase of outcome research had a
profound, if indirect and diffuse, effect on social work practice and
thinking (Smith, 1987). For years we have found agreement on one
thing among experienced practitioners in this field; they may dis-
agree about much, but they all say that 'treatment' does not work.
Some, more dispiritingly, say that nothing else works either. What
basis is there in research for these views, and are they justified?

It has become a truism, rightly enough, that the 'medical model'
has been discredited in work with individual offenders. It is not
always clear, however, just what the 'medical model' is, or was.
From the writings of the 1960s, it is possible to find occasionally
what looks like the model in relatively pure form: for instance, the
much-cited article by Winnicott (1962), in which she implies that
offending is a symptom of an illness. This is, indeed, a difficult position to defend, at least for the great majority of cases, if it is taken to
mean that offences are involuntary acts (like sneezes) rather than acts
which are in some sense voluntary and chosen – that is, the offender
could have *not* done what he or she did. This strong version of the
medical model seems so out of line with everyday understanding of
offending that it is hard to believe that it can ever have been taken
literally by practitioners. Indeed, there is plenty of evidence that it
was not (e.g. Davies, 1969). But it seems quite likely that a weaker
version was influential in practice, a version which allowed or
encouraged workers to feel that they knew better than their clients
what was good for them. In particular, both Winnicott, and Foren
and Bailey (1968) encouraged probation officers to think that the
exercise of authority over their clients would necessarily be for their
clients' benefit, whatever the clients might think about it. This is the
kind of thinking lucidly criticised by Bottoms and McWilliams
(1979) and Raynor (1978); it led Bottoms and McWilliams towards
their 'non-treatment paradigm', in which 'appropriate help' is sub-
stituted for treatment as an aim of social work with offenders – a sub-
stitution with which we entirely agree.

All the same, it is often not clear what the 'treatment' the outcomes of which were evaluated in the first phase of research, actually consisted of, and this needs to be remembered in considering how the research influenced practice. By about 1976 the belief was widespread, certainly in the probation service, that whatever else social work with offenders might achieve, it was not very good at stopping its clients from offending. It was not much comfort that the same seemed to be true of other approaches – residential care, for example. This belief was based on a number of pieces of research which together seemed to add up to the message that 'nothing works'. There was a considerable background influence, as there often is, from the United States; the work of Robert Martinson and his colleagues in particular encouraged this gloomy view (Martinson, 1974). Their work, which was widely disseminated not only in the probation service but also in the prison service, suggested, on the basis of a large-scale review of experimental evaluations of 'correctional treatment', that there were no grounds for preferring any one approach to any other: all produced equally bad results. This was the climate in which the British research that came out at about the same time was received.

Some of this research concerned residential care, and could be, and was, used to argue for support of young offenders in the community rather than in institutions, particularly in community homes with education on the premises (Thorpe *et al*, 1980). But the research could have been used in other ways. For instance, Ian Sinclair's work on probation hostels (Sinclair, 1971), and Anne Dunlop's and the Dartington group's research on approved schools (the forerunners of CHEs) all suggested that there was no encouraging evidence that these institutions reduced delinquency (Dunlop, 1975; Millham, Bullock and Cherrett, 1975). There were, however, some differences in reconviction rates, and, more interestingly, there were significant variations in the rates of offending and absconding between institutions. That is, some of the hostels and schools were doing better than others in providing accommodation and encouraging at least a remission of offending. In a different climate, this could have led to further research, along the lines suggested by Sinclair, on what produced the differences; but this important question was neglected in favour of an overall negative reception of the results. The work of Cornish and Clarke (1975), which was more limited in scope and more negative in its findings, certainly encouraged this gloomy interpretation: they found not only that there was no difference in reconvictions between a 'traditional' and a 'therapeutic community' approved school regime, but that the results suggested something worse than failure – the possibility that these schools actually created delinquency.

In the meantime, research on social work in the community, specifically on the work of the probation service, was not, unfortunately, proving much more encouraging. Martin Davies (1969; 1974a) suggested that probation officers might be able to help young offenders in various ways, but the best results were with clients who arguably needed help least in the first place, and there was no positive evidence that probation could bring about a reduction in offending. Worse still, the elaborate and ambitious Home Office experiment known as IMPACT (Folkard, Smith and Smith, 1976) concluded that offenders supervised more intensively than usual were more likely to get worse than to get better, and did worse if anything than those subjected to only routine supervision. The probation service was thus, on the face of it, deprived not only of any ground on which to argue for more resources, but of the main traditional justification for its existence. Before IMPACT, probation officers sometimes argued that 'we're not a social work agency, we're a crime prevention agency'; after IMPACT, this claim, perhaps never very plausible, could hardly be treated seriously.

Nevertheless, the outcome research of the early 1970s was capable of being interpreted in other ways than 'Nothing works'. There were, for example, encouraging results on reconvictions for men leaving prison after 'extended contact' with prison-based probation officers; like IMPACT, this research was based on a rigorous experimental design (Shaw, 1974). There was evidence that social work in schools could have good results in the reduction of delinquency (Rose and Marshall, 1974), and that prisoners released on parole had better than predicted reconviction rates (Nuttall *et al*, 1977). As we noted above, the research on approved schools and probation hostels at least suggested that some kinds of residential social work were better than others, and even IMPACT indicated that there were differences in the response of different types of client to different 'treatment' approaches. This has recently led some writers, for example Ken Pease, who worked for the Home Office Research Unit in the 1970s, to argue that the pessimistic conclusions drawn from this research were not necessarily justified (Pease, 1984).

Pease points out that the pioneering work of Truax and Carkhuff (1967), which suggested that what social workers thought they were doing might be less important than how they did it, was never followed up. In fact there has been no large-scale research solely concerned with the outcomes of social work with offenders since IMPACT, although the IMPACT authors themselves suggested ways in which their work might be carried on. The reasons for this neglect are no doubt complex, but it is reasonable to think that one important factor was a change in the political climate. The 1970s, as Hall *et al* (1978) convincingly argue, saw the start of the breakdown of the post-war consensus on 'welfare', and this applied with particular force to work with offenders: 'law and order' had become an important political issue by the time of the 1979 election which ushered in the era of 'Thatcherism'. Both in Britain and in the United States, a 'neo-conservative', anti-welfare lobby was gaining in power and confidence, and the defenders of the traditional values of the welfare state were no longer certain of their ground. The negative interpretation of the outcome research found a ready reception among this newly powerful political constituency; and the potential opposition was weak and divided.

From the late 1970s on, then, research into social work with offenders took a very different turn, and this both reflected and was reflected in the way practitioners thought about their work. Rather than looking at the effect of social work intervention on the lives or behaviour of individual offenders, research became concerned with the impact social work might have on the criminal justice system. Indeed, influencing the workings of the local criminal justice system has come to be seen by many practitioners and social work managers as the main justification for maintaining a social work presence within the system. It is even sometimes argued that what social workers actually do when face to face with clients hardly matters (because nothing will work better than anything else). This is certainly not a view which we share, but it is worth tracing how it has developed.

One important factor in the emergence of this rather nihilistic position has undoubtedly been the outcome research described above. But another, rather different kind of influence appeared in the late 1970s and early 1980s in the work of David Thorpe and his colleagues at Lancaster University (Thorpe *et al*, 1980). While emphatically not saying that it did not matter what social work practice with juvenile offenders consisted of, Thorpe argued that, however good their intentions, social workers often drew young offenders unnecessarily into the criminal justice system by excessive and premature intervention. Using the development of intermediate treatment in the 1970s as an example, Thorpe argued that the original intentions of the legislation (the 1969 Children and Young Persons Act) had failed to be realised in practice, because social workers, inspired by the doctrine of 'needology', provided intermediate treatment in a thoughtless and undiscriminating way. Instead of confining it to those for whom (supposedly) it was originally intended – relatively persistent and serious offenders at risk of care or custody – social workers became entranced by the notion of 'preventive' intermediate treatment. This had a number of results: the group of serious offenders who most needed it received, in many cases, no community-based service at all, and were confined in increasing numbers in care or custodial establishments; and juveniles who might not have committed any offence were treated to the benefits of outdoor pursuits and other forms of 'preventive' work which, to say the least, were not always clearly linked with delinquency. This was more than a problem of the mis-allocation or misuse of resources; Thorpe and his colleagues also showed that there was at least a tendency for such preventive work to channel young people into the criminal justice and care systems, rather than divert them from it. The important point here was not whether preventive work could or could not be successful; indeed, the evidence of Rose and Marshall (1974) suggested that in some circumstances it could achieve the desired results. What mattered was that this work was being done by statutory agencies – mainly social services departments – whose work was inevitably closely linked both to court disposals and to the child care system. The stigmatising effects of perceived failure would have been less damaging if the work had been undertaken by agencies less closely linked with these formal systems, along the lines described for recent social crime prevention projects in Chapter 3. But as it was, the 'failure' of preventive work could deprive both social workers and courts of the option of using intermediate treatment in a diversionary way, and leave no alternative to removal from home.

In Cohen's (1985) terms, this account is a variety of 'We blew it': the intentions were good, the legislation was alright, but the implementation went wrong – in this case, because of the lack of a clear (and restrictive) policy on intermediate treatment, and the naïve enthusiasm of social workers for a new and apparently more benign system. In our view, while Thorpe's version of the intentions of the 1969 legislation can be and has been disputed (Pratt, 1987), this analysis still has a good deal to offer. At the most general level, it is useful in reminding social workers that they need to take into account the impact their decisions may have on other decisions, made by other people elsewhere in the criminal justice sytem. For instance, a supervision order imposed on a juvenile appearing in court for the first time may well foreclose the possibility of a further order should the juvenile re-offend: over-intervention (with the best of intentions) could increase the likelihood of a custodial sentence later on. In fact, this sort of strategic thinking needs little defence: although much criticised by advocates of a more open, optimistic, developmental form of IT for its 'penal' emphasis, the so-called 'Lancaster model' has now, in England and Wales but not in Scotland, become widely accepted as the 'new orthodoxy'. This has not, of course, led to unqualified enthusiasm for it in all quarters; but it is undoubtedly one of the bases for much successful current practice in IT.

The work of Thorpe and his colleagues preceded some larger-scale research on juvenile justice systems and the social workers' contribution to their management. For example, NACRO's Juvenile Offenders Team (later the Juvenile Crime Section) undertook extensive monitoring of the effects of the 1983 DHSS initiative, often known by its Circular number, LAC 83(3), which encouraged the expansion

of IT as an alternative to custody; NACRO also promoted and supported local monitoring efforts (NACRO, 1988). Another initiative,
more narrowly concerned with monitoring local criminal justice decisions, came from a private company, Social Information Systems
(SIS). The most prominent figures in this were two leading academics in the field, Norman Tutt and Henri Giller, who had been identified respectively with the development of the 'Lancaster model' and
with the 'back to justice' movement. This movement had, in the late
1970s, been strongly critical of the injustices which could arise from
the unfettered use of executive discretionary powers by 'welfare'
agencies, and had advocated a return to proportionality between the
offence and the disposal and other principles of justice in the juvenile
courts (Morris *et al*, 1980). Retaining a sceptical view of the place of
social work in juvenile justice, but not, like some 'back to justice'
advocates, denying that it had a place, SIS has worked with several
local authorities to help them develop information and monitoring
systems and thus have a rational basis for defining their juvenile justice policy. SIS has also highlighted the differences in cautioning and
sentencing patterns between different areas (Richardson, 1988).

Part of the value of the work of NACRO, and the central theme of
SIS, which is reflected in many areas in local systems monitoring, is
that they have consistently stressed the importance of accurate information about the workings of the juvenile justice process: how many
juveniles are cautioned, how many prosecuted; what is the proportionate use of different sentences by a local court; what are the characteristics of offenders on whom these sentences are imposed (in
terms of previous convictions, for instance, but also of race and gender); what is the contribution of social work agencies, measured primarily by social inquiry report recommendations. There is a good
deal of evidence that this kind of careful monitoring of the workings
of local systems does enable policy to be formed and implemented far
more effectively than in the past, with the possibility, at least in some
areas, of the creation of 'custody-free zones' such as Basingstoke
(Rutherford, 1986).

This sort of monitoring has also made it possible to identify more
clearly some hitherto neglected issues in juvenile justice – for
example, the way in which young black people may become victims
of the institutionalised racism of the system, and be underrepresented
in IT projects while being overrepresented in custody (NACRO,
1986; NACRO, 1988). Similarly, monitoring can reveal any consistent differences in the ways in which girls and young women are
treated compared with boys and young men. The considerable overall reduction in the use of custody for juveniles, from a peak of 7,700
(6.8 % of all those cautioned or prosecuted) in 1981 to 4,100 (4.1 %)
in 1987 (Home Office, 1988a), almost certainly owes something to
the more sensitive tactical awareness of system factors which many

social workers and probation officers now bring to their work – an issue to which we return later.

We want, however, to make it clear that we do not subscribe to the view that systems monitoring and management are the only appropriate aims for social work in criminal justice. The risk of exclusive concentration on system goals is that social work itself – the work that takes place when workers meet their clients – may be devalued or forgotten. In a political climate which emphasises cost-effectiveness, value for money, efficiency and other totems of monetarism, it is tempting to evaluate the work of a social work agency by system effects alone, disregarding questions about the quality and outcomes of social work intervention with individual clients. The latter are hard to measure, often intangible or long-term, not readily susceptible to computer analysis; the former are capable of being turned into hard facts and figures, neatly tabulated and apparently providing a basis for hard-nosed managerial scrutiny. Since the Home Office's 'Statement of National Objectives and Priorities' for the probation service (Home Office, 1984), there has been a clear tendency for the work of probation teams to be assessed in this way; and, by a rather different route, the Association for Juvenile Justice (AJJ), an organisation which would claim to represent the radical wing of juvenile justice practice, has arrived at much the same position.

In some versions of AJJ thinking, 'welfare' has become a dirty word; the best thing social workers can do with young offenders is to leave them alone. Since this is not always practicable, it is more important to persuade the courts that you are doing something constructive than actually to do it. The AJJ position is satirically set out by Pitts (1988, pp 90–2); allowing for some exaggeration, his account of the 'minimalist radicalism' of the AJJ is broadly accurate. Behind it lie the negative interpretations of the 1970s outcome research and the insistence by the critics of naïve conceptions of social work as the promotion of welfare on the centrality of systems thinking; but, more generally, this kind of thinking reflects the influence of the labelling perspective or social reaction theory, which we described earlier as the single most important influence of formal criminology on social work. Social workers are certainly not to be blamed for doing what they are so often accused of never doing – attending to the insights of social science. Nevertheless, we believe that it is still important to consider questions about the quality of social work practice; and that it does matter what social workers do when actually working with offenders. This is not an academic question; for reasons to be explored later, we think it has an immediate political urgency.

In concluding this review of the research which has been most important in shaping conceptions of social work with offenders in the last two decades, we want to draw attention to two points. Firstly, the work of Thorpe and his colleagues needs to be sharply distinguished

from that of the more exclusively systems-oriented work which succeeded it. Thorpe *et al* (1980) employed a very partial form of systems analysis which is likely to seem primitive compared with the
sophisticated versions which developed in the 1980s. On the other
hand, they were highly prescriptive about what kinds of face-to-face
practice with young offenders were likely to be most appropriate and
useful; and their suggestions, as developed particularly by Denman
(1982), have been influential in both IT and probation practice in
day-centre contexts, and arguably in recent government statements
on the desirable content of social work with offenders. We discuss
the implications of this below. Secondly, we are happy to note the
reappearance in some recent research writings of a concern with the
nature and outcomes of social work practice. Pease (1984, 1985a) has
advocated renewed attention to outcome research; and Raynor
(1988), among others, has combined attention to system effects with
an interest in individual change in the clients in his evaluation of a
probation day centre in South Wales. Raynor is concerned with system questions such as whether the centre, offering a form of
'enhanced' probation, was dealing with the 'right' clients – that is
those genuinely at risk of a custodial sentence. But he is interested
not only in the traditional individual change measure of reconvictions
but also in the extent to which the centre's clients felt that their
personal problems and difficulties had been alleviated by the work
attempted at the centre. This seems to provide a model of how
research might develop, particularly in IT, where little attention has
been paid to outcomes for individuals, except in local, do-it-yourself
evaluations (Children's Society Advisory Committee, 1988). It is
pleasant to be able to conclude by noting that the results of Raynor's
evaluation are generally encouraging: social work can make a difference, in the right direction.

Working with adult offenders: towards punishment in the community

As a generalisation, the biggest single problem faced by successive
governments in penal policy over the past twenty years has been the
size of the prison population. As we showed in the previous chapter,
this has shown a consistent and alarming tendency to grow – not
altogether steadily, but still with an unmistakable upward trend.
And although there have been differences in emphasis in the ways in
which governments have responded to this 'crisis' – with, for
example, noticeably less being said about reducing the prison population and more about the need to build new prisons during Leon
Brittan's period of tenure at the Home Office – there has also been a
remarkable consistency about the general strategy. This has been to

encourage courts to make more use of an increasing range of 'alternatives' to custody, which have been provided in successive pieces of criminal justice legislation; and this legislative change has been accompanied by exhortations to courts to restrict the use of custody to relatively serious offenders, for whom, on retributive grounds or because of the need to protect the public, there is no alternative to incarceration.

In the previous chapter we showed why it is far from clear that this strategy has been the right one: 'alternatives' to custody tend to be used in practice as alternatives to something else; and the aim of reducing the average daily prison population could be better achieved by legislation to reduce sentence lengths than by a proliferation of new non-custodial measures. Our concern here, however, is with the implications this policy has had for the development of social work with adult offenders; in England and Wales, this principally means the work of the probation service. In Scotland, the issues are somewhat different, because despite an even higher proportion of the population being in prison, there has until recently been little social work activity in this field, since in the absence of a separate probation service adult offenders have generally not been a high priority group for social work departments (Gill, 1988).

One consistent theme over the past twenty years has been the need for the probation service to change the practice of supervision in the community to make it tighter and more demanding. This expectation was first made explicit with the introduction of parole in 1968, following the Criminal Justice Act. Because prisoners released on parole licence were still legally serving a prison sentence, and had generally committed more serious offences than the clients with whom the probation service had usually dealt, there was a new emphasis on public accountability and the need for clear procedures and effective controls (Cooper, 1987). In practice, however, it quickly became clear the probation officers were not supervising parolees any more tightly or rigorously than they would supervise people on probation, whose legal status was very different (Davies, 1974b; Parker and Williams, 1976); the new legal category did not produce a new style of practice. Not for the last time, the practice of probation officers revealed itself as somewhat at odds with the apparent expectations of the legislators.

This is in one sense not surprising, because a striking feature of the growth of the probation service has always been its *ad hoc*, pragmatic nature. There was no special reason why probation should have been thought the obvious agency to take on parole supervision, just as there had been no special reason for thinking that it should undertake social work in prisons, a duty it had begun in 1966. In both cases, despite some publicly expressed reservations, the probation service was given these new duties mainly because it was there (Advisory Council on the Treatment of Offenders, 1963); this was easier than creating a new agency, and any ensuing grumbles were unlikely to be loud enough to lead to the fall of governments.

The same consideration applies with added force to the introduction of community service orders following the 1972 Criminal Justice Act. Community service means a form of compulsory, unpaid labour; at first sight this might seem remote from the traditional concern of the probation service to 'advise, assist and befriend'. But in fact, apart from occasional mutterings about labour camps, there was little contemporary resistance among probation officers to this new element in their work. One reason was that the 'philosophy' of community service was defined in such broad terms as to be capable of appealing to almost anyone. Barbara Wootton, who chaired the Advisory Council which first recommended community service in 1970, later said (Wootton, 1978) that she had always been slightly ashamed of this 'attempt to curry favour with everybody', but it was undoubtedly a major element in the success of community service not only with courts but within the probation service. The Advisory Council noted that community service could be seen simply as an alternative to a short prison sentence; as a way of bringing the principle of reparation into the penal system; as a way of making the punishment fit the crime; and as potentially rehabilitative for offenders, who might discover new possibilities in their lives through working alongside non-offenders, and through contact with the needy or dependent in the community. As Pease (1983) noted, this was less a philosophy than a refusal to state a philosophy. It meant that probation officers could welcome as an opportunity for 'new careers' for offenders a measure which magistrates could regard as a modern version of the stocks.

The very success of community service with sentencers meant, however, that the humanistic or rehabilitative view of it became harder and harder to sustain. It depended on the availability of work for offenders in the human services – with the elderly and handicapped, for example. As the sheer number of community service orders grew, and as unemployment rates increased through the late 1970s and early 1980s, the scope for providing work of this sort for offenders steadily contracted, and community service was subjected, in Ken Pease's terms, to 'chain-gangisation'; the work became almost exclusively manual, menial and arduous. One effect of this has been the virtual exclusion of women from community service; as was shown in the previous chapter, women are overrepresented on probation, compared with the total number of women sentenced, but seriously underrepresented in the figures for community service. The trend towards an increasingly punitive conception of community service has, however, been approved by the Government: the national standards for community service issued by the Home Office in 1988 make it clear that hard manual labour is to be considered a normal element of this sentence. That is, it is to be conceived largely in punitive terms; and this creates a problem for probation officers who want to argue that punishment in the community is alien to the essential character and traditions of the service. The Trojan horse is already within the gates, although perhaps not obviously so, since community service has become a highly specialised area of probation practice which does not impinge directly on the day-to-day work of most probation officers. In Scotland, where community service was introduced later and has developed more slowly, it will be interesting to see whether social work departments can resist, as some at least are trying to do, the erosion of a conception of community service as something other, or at least more, than punishment.

The second important innovation for the probation service of the 1972 Act was the establishment of day training centres. These, like community service, were to be set up on an experimental basis, and were to provide a resource for inadequate offenders lacking in social skills and in stable elements in their lives such as jobs, homes and families. (Community service, by contrast, was thought to be particularly suitable for offenders with jobs and enough stability to give them a reasonable chance of completing the order by turning up on time.) Four day training centres were set up in 1973, in London, Pontypridd, Liverpool and Sheffield; but, compared with community service, there was little Government enthusiasm for them (perhaps because of their higher cost and narrower appeal), and the research on their success which the Home Office intended to conduct, was never completed or published. Offenders could be required to attend these centres as a condition of a probation order for a period of up to sixty days, providing an obvious parallel with the way in which IT conditions came to be incorporated into supervision orders. The centres gradually developed a characteristic style of work, based on social skills training in groups; the Sheffield centre in particular became one of the testing grounds for the 'social skills and personal problem-solving' approach of Philip Priestley and his colleagues (Priestley *et al*, 1977).

In 1974, the report of the Advisory Council on the Penal System on young adult offenders (the 'Younger Report') advocated a greatly strengthened form of supervision in the community in which the elements of surveillance and discipline would have clear priority over those of help and support. This 'supervision and control order' would not require the consent of the offender, and would include powers for probation officers to arrange for the subjects of the order to be detained for seventy-two hours if, in the officer's opinion, they seemed likely to be about to commit an offence. This particular proposal was strongly opposed by the probation service and never implemented, but it showed one developing strand of thought about the service's role; and, although the Younger Committee's recommendations were not acted on directly, it is interesting that several of their proposals, including the creation of a single form of custody for young offenders, have re-surfaced since, in some of the provisions of the 1982 and 1988 Criminal Justice Acts (in the latter, the creation of a single category of young offenders' institution).

As the 1970s progressed, many probation managers began to worry about the declining use of probation, and to ponder the implications of the increasing use of community service. One conclusion that could be, and was, drawn from this trend was that the probation order lacked credibility and appeal because it lacked the features that made community service attractive – a punitive element, guarantees about the length and nature of the contact the service would have with the offender, and some assurance that breaches of the order would lead to a return to court. Bill Jordan (1983) suggested that this line of reasoning meant that probation should become more like prison – no longer a modified form of liberty, but a modified form of imprisonment. This position was put clearly by Martin Davies in an address to a Chief Probation Officers' conference, advocating ' noncustodial disposal that will be seen not only as an acceptable option to prison, but as a punitive, retributive and controlling facility in its own right' (Davies, 1982). A number of probation services followed this advice, most famously in the case of Kent, whose 'Probation Control Unit', in sharp contrast to the day training centres, deliberately emphasised containment and discipline at the expense of an individualised helping agenda for its 'clients'.

In other areas the probation service began to establish new day centres, or adapt existing ones which had been set up on a purely voluntary basis (Fairhead, 1981), to provide a way of 'enhancing' the probation order by introducing a tighter structure and thus, it was hoped, increasing its appeal to sentencers. Largely drawing on the day training centres as models rather than on the Kent variant, the practice grew in a number of areas, with Home Office support, of encouraging courts to include in orders a new condition of attendance for a specified period at a 'day centre', which meant in practice whatever groupwork facility the local service had been able to set up. Unfortunately and embarrassingly, this practice turned out, in the judgement of the Law Lords in the 1981 case of Cullen *v*. Rogers, to be illegal: the judgement was that the provision for such additional requirements was confined to the four original day training centres, and that its extension without legislative warrant gave the probation service excessive discretionary powers. The Government hastened to rectify this position, by incorporating into Schedule XI of the 1982 Criminal Justice Act measures which in effect legalised the practices which had developed before the Cullen *v*. Rogers case.

Since then, day centres, as the main available means of strengthening probation orders, have been at the heart of debates within the probation service about how, and indeed whether, supervision in the community should be made more intensive. Many practitioners, and their Trades Union voice in NAPO, have expressed worries about the use of any additional requirements in probation orders, viewing this as an indication of a drift towards a more controlling role for the service (e.g. Drakeford, 1983; Spencer, 1988; NAPO, 1985), and expressing scepticism about the possible impact that probation officers can have on the use of custody (e.g. NAPO, 1988). Bullock and Tildesley (1984) found that in the area they studied many officers felt that any elements in probation orders beyond the basic requirements to keep in touch with the supervising officer should be voluntary: for example, if a client had a drinking problem, and the probation service was running a relevant group, the client could be invited to attend, but this should not be built into the order (cf. McLoone, Oulds and Morris, 1987). Other officers disagreed, and the effect was that in this probation service at least sentencers were presented with an image of confusion, uncertainty and conflict.

A similar controversy on a national scale, and one which has acquired immediate relevance in the context of the Government's most recent statements on the probation service's purpose, concerns 'tracking'. The scheme of most concern to the service and to NAPO in particular, because seconded probation officers were involved in it, has been a project in Leeds which aimed to provide alternatives to care and custody for juveniles. (An adult 'tracking' project has been set up since – and is about to change its name to substitute 'intensive supervision' for 'tracking'.) Part of the work of the juvenile project involved the intensive supervision (by volunteers) of young people awaiting a place in a groupwork programme or remanded on bail: they might be expected to see their 'trackers' daily, or to keep in frequent contact with them by telephone. At the National Intermediate Treatment Conference at Sheffield in 1985, one of the present writers was an innocent (but rather exposed) bystander during a vigorous and highly public argument between the General Secretary of NAPO and the probation officer in charge of the Leeds project about the ethics and appropriateness of tracking as a probation activity. One of the ironies of this argument was that the probation service appeared as the guardian of 'pure' social work values, in which, supposedly, tracking could have no place, against local and national voluntary organisations whose traditions, on the face of it, were much more remote from anything smacking of overt control than those of the probation service. The recurrent ambiguity in probation work (crudely, 'care or control') was given a further, perhaps unexpected twist.

This particular argument has been given fresh urgency by the publication of the Government's Green Paper on 'Punishment, Custody and the Community' (Home Office, 1988b) and the associated circular

'Tackling Offending – An Action Plan' (Home Office, 1988c). A naïve observer might find it surprising that the latter, concerned with supervision in the community for young adult offenders, has been circulated not only to probation areas, the police, magistrates' clerks and the like – those most obviously involved in criminal justice – but also to voluntary organisations concerned with children and young people like NCH (National Children's Home), Save the Children Fund and the Intermediate Treatment Fund. What have these organisations to do with the traditional area of work of the probation service? The answer is that a recurring theme of the 'Action Plan', to parody it only slightly, is that the namby-pamby, queasily liberal probation service must swallow its qualms and learn from the tough-minded, hard-nosed initiatives taken with juvenile offenders by these charitable (and in some cases religious) organisations. The unease often expressed by people considering social work as a job, that the probation service is too concerned with social control, and that they might therefore be happier and more independent outside the state apparatus, working for a voluntary organisation, is thus seen to be misplaced: the advocates of social control are in the voluntary sector, and they are eager to put their experience with juveniles at the service of the state as the emphasis shifts to young adult offenders (Children's Society, 1989; White, 1988).

Something like this is, at any rate, the view of NAPO; and, as its response to the Green Paper (NAPO, 1988) indicates, it is concerned not only with the way in which voluntary sector initiatives may be used as a precedent and model for a more controlling and disciplinary style of probation practice, but with the possibility that the involvement of voluntary organisations may be the thin end of the wedge of privatisation. There are certainly strong hints in the Green Paper that some of its proposals, especially 'tagging', which might be seen as the electronic version of tracking, could be handled by private concerns. Indeed, the Government's message to the probation service in the Green Paper is fairly clear: if the service will not adapt its work to encompass the proposed new measures of 'punishment in the community', the Government will find someone else who will.

In the conclusion of the next chapter, we discuss in some detail how the probation service might best respond to this implied threat; now, we want to suggest two things. Firstly, that NAPO's suspicion of voluntary sector involvement may be misplaced. The kind of inter-agency work that the Green Paper and the Action Plan (especially the latter) envisage is closely modelled on initiatives in work with juveniles which have developed since 1983 (of which more below) and have been encouraged by NACRO in particular. There is no special reason to think that these developments are necessarily associated with privatisation, in the sense of the introduction of the profit motive into the provision of services for young offenders. The involvement of private enterprise has been confined to training, research and consultancy, and this is not a new phenomenon, or even a 'Thatcherite' one. Secondly, it seems necessary to distinguish between those aspects of the Green Paper and the Action Plan which are compatible with 'enhanced' probation practice (of the kind which the service has (since the late 1970s at least) shown itself perfectly willing to undertake, and those which are not. Our view, despite the difficulty, noted above, in arguing that punishment in the community is essentially alien to a service which runs a community service, is that there is a good deal in the Government's proposals which is in line with a developing, and widely approved, practice; and that opposition should be directed against the ideas which would bring into supervision in the community an element which can only be defined as punitive, in the sense of deliberately irksome and restrictive. Some restrictions are widely recognised as compatible with the aim of helping offenders (Raynor, 1985); others are inimical to it. The problem, which we address at the end of the next chapter, is to decide which are which.

6 Developments in social work (ii): Juvenile offenders

For some time now it has been customary in accounts of social work with juvenile offenders to take the late 1960s as the starting point for analysis of recent developments in juvenile criminal justice. The logic of this is clear: in England and Wales, after prolonged academic and political discussion and two White Papers, there emerged, in the 1969 Children and Young Persons Act, a measure which promised radical reform of the system of juvenile justice which had been in place almost since the beginning of the century. In Scotland, the Social Work (Scotland) Act of 1968 abolished the existing juvenile court system and replaced it with a system of Children's Hearings, which were explicitly to be concerned with the welfare of children and young people and not with their punishment. Taken together, the two pieces of legislation have been seen as the high-water mark of reform in the field of juvenile delinquency; they represented, apparently, the triumph of 'welfare' as the dominant ideology.

But, as is well known, what actually happened in England and Wales was very different from events in Scotland. There, the Children's Hearings were successfully established, and in their wake came a set of services for troublesome and troubled children – the two categories were not treated as separate – which were defined by the ideology of child care. Although there has been criticism and debate about whether this system is the right one (Morris and McIsaac, 1978; Martin, Fox and Murray, 1981), it has withstood these challenges, and as one result the pattern of social work services for juvenile offenders (up to the age of 16), and the associated policy arguments, have been very different in Scotland from those in England and Wales. The distinctive character of the Scottish practice, and in particular of Intermediate Treatment (IT) in Scotland, is succinctly described in the IT Resource Centre's Review (IT Resource Centre, 1986). It does not form part of any child care legislation in Scotland, and has thus

developed as a purely discretionary response to young people's needs by
social workers and others. . . . In many parts of Scotland, IT owes its
origins to the individual initiative of social workers or youth workers . . .
practitioner-led initiatives have emphasised neighbourhood-based
approaches to IT, voluntary attendance and an avoidance of labelling the
young people who attend. Departmental initiatives, in contrast, have
focussed more on providing intensive alternatives to residential care or
custody for those young people who are already caught up in the system
(ITRC, 1986, p 3).

The review goes on to note that there are very few young people
under 16 in prison department establishments in Scotland; thus, in
so far as IT has recently been encouraged to develop in a more
focused way, it is as an alternative to residential care rather than to
custody. It is clear from the ITRC Review and from other sources
(Strathcyde Regional Council, 1987) that IT in Scotland has retained
a different emphasis and style from its southern counterpart; and
that most of those interested in this field in Scotland thoroughly support the continuation of this difference. We can summarise the characteristics of IT in Scotland as follows: compared with England and
Wales, it has retained a preventive focus; it is concerned to avoid
labelling and stigma; it is broad-based and relatively diffuse in its
aims and in the range of young people it deals with; it is not exclusively a social work activity but also involves community and youth
workers; it has always entailed a mix of statutory and voluntary activity; and, perhaps most importantly, it has an air of optimism and
developmental enthusiasm not always evident further south. This is
not to say that everything in the Scottish garden is roses; as mentioned above, the fate of young adults (over the age of 16) before the
Scottish courts is often bleak. Nevertheless, it seemed reasonable to
Scottish practitioners that they should not entirely follow the path
taken by IT in England; they have sought to retain the open and diffuse approach from which, south of the border, many IT workers
have for the last ten years been trying to escape. Much English IT,
the ITRC Review suggests, has 'repudiated its social work roots in
favour of a "new realism" ' (IT Resource Centre, 1986, p 3). Is this
true, and, if so, how has it come about?

The rise of the 'new orthodoxy'

The prehistory and history of the 1969 Act have been written a
number of times, and we do not intend to repeat the tale here (for
a variety of accounts, see Thorpe *et al*, 1980; Harris and Webb,
1987; Bottoms, 1974; Pitts, 1988). The broad outlines of it are clear
and agreed, although there is some dispute about detail, particularly about the use that was envisaged for IT (Pratt, 1987). The

legislation, like that in Scotland, was intended to be substantially decriminalising and diversionary, and to substitute the principles and practices of child care for those of criminal justice in dealing with juvenile offenders. 'Decarceration', in the sense of reducing the use of institutions by developing community services, was less clearly a part of the programme; the aim was to transform the existing institutions, turning detention centres into child care establishments, rather than to close them. Even if fully implemented, the Act might have had less radical effects than has sometimes been claimed; it was its commitment to welfarism which was radical, not its deinstitutionalising thrust. But it was never fully implemented: the detention centres and borstals remained as before, and the new system, far from replacing the old, was grafted on to it. The result was confusion and uncertainty, an apparent loss of faith, by courts, in social workers, and by social workers in themselves, and, in the decade following the Act, a rapid increase in the absolute and proportionate use of custody for juveniles. Rutherford (1983) wrote that

> The 1970s were a particularly dismal decade. If we take the number of sentenced receptions in 1971 as equal to 100, in 1981 receptions of persons 21 and over were 137; those of persons aged 17–20 were 166; and those of persons aged 14–16 were 247.

Rutherford went on to predict, like many other commentators, that the 1982 Criminal Justice Act would make things even worse.

This awareness of the increase in the use of prison department custody for juveniles was in fact relatively new. The received Conservative wisdom of the 1970s was that the trouble with the 1969 Act was that it gave social workers too much power, at the expense of sentencers, and that the consequence was that young thugs were getting away with it. In fact the only part of the legislation in which there had been a substantial shift of power was in relation to care orders: sentencers lost the power to determine that a juvenile should be sent to an Approved School; under a care order the placement of the juvenile was a matter for the discretion of the social services department. The 'Justice for Children' movement (Morris *et al*, 1980) also concentrated, but for different reasons, on this (statistically marginal) aspect of the system, arguing that social workers' unfettered discretion to apply welfare criteria in deciding what to do with juvenile offenders meant that the principle of proportionality between the offence and the disposal had been lost. In the interests of justice, it should be reintroduced. Thorpe *et al* (1980), while acknowledging that the use of custody was a problem, also concentrated mainly on care orders in criminal cases, arguing that many of these were made unnecessarily and unjustly, and that their effect was often to channel juveniles further into the very system of criminal justice from which the legislation was supposed to protect them.

Thus care, not custody, was the central issue for reformers, in whatever direction they hoped the reform would take place. This was odd in one sense, since the use of care orders in criminal cases had in fact peaked as early as 1974; 6,600 juveniles were sentenced to care in that year, compared with 2,900 in 1981, the peak year for custody (Home Office, 1983; the counting rules had changed in the meantime, but not, it seems, enough to distort the picture grossly). But in another way, the focus on care orders made good pragmatic and political sense; it offered a prospect of achieving something like the almost legendary 'decarceration' managed by Jerome Miller in Massachusetts (Rutherford, 1986), since the implementation of a care order in effect came out of a local criminal justice budget; there was a local financial motive for change. The early work of David Thorpe and his colleagues was with small local authorities without their own community homes with education; the development of alternatives to care was often supported because, among other things, it would save the ratepayers' money. This was important to many authorities in the late 1970s; it is useful to remember that monetarism was not a Thatcherite invention. The trouble was that the preferred alternative to care might be custody; this would save the ratepayers' money still more effectively, since the prison department makes no local charge. From file studies in some areas, we are aware that this option was sometimes consciously taken, as when social workers recommended a borstal sentence on a juvenile subject to a care order, and immediately proceeded to discharge the care order, thankfully handing over the responsibility for their clients to the probation service. Even without this overt cynicism, there is little doubt that the move from care to custody did emerge as a trend in areas in which no planned and properly funded IT system existed to provide support for juvenile offenders in the community, and also, more frustratingly, in areas in which it proved very difficult to influence sentencers to move away from punitive habits. Variations in sentencing between courts have posed a long-standing problem for penal policy analysts (Tarling, 1979; Richardson, 1988); there are stories of failure as well as of success, though, understandably, the latter tend to be better publicised.

By the early 1980s, the view of IT associated with David Thorpe and others was becoming established as the 'new orthodoxy'. Instead of the diffuse, potentially 'net-widening' practice of preventive work with those 'at risk', IT should be aimed specifically at the relatively persistent and serious offenders who were at risk of removal from home (which by this time meant removal to custody). This success was certainly not universally welcomed; Pitts (1988) explores some of the reasons why it might be, and was, resisted. Among these reasons was the fact that the approach seemed to be approved by the first government of Margaret Thatcher. The White Paper 'Young Offenders' (Home Office, 1980) in some ways reflected the criticisms of the 1969 Act with which the Conservative party had long been associated, with its suggestions of some form of residential care order to ensure that the social workers' supposed laxity was controlled. It also reflected a contemporary preoccupation in its enthusiasm for the 'short, sharp shock' – a brief period in a detention centre which was to be made as deliberately unpleasant as possible. But the White Paper faced both ways: while extolling the virtues of punitive regimes, it also encouraged an increase in the use of cautions and promised the development of a wider range of non-custodial measures. Similar contradictions appear in the subsequent legislation, the 1982 Criminal Justice Act.

This Act gave magistrates a wider range of both custodial and non-custodial options. It has been widely recognised that it should be seen as a compromise between the long established Conservative concern to be seen to take a tough line on law and order and a more pragmatic interest in keeping juvenile (and adult) offenders out of custody where possible. Thus, it introduced for the first time a statutory basis for the provision of social inquiry reports (SIRs), and a requirement that sentencers should only impose a custodial sentence if they were satisfied that no other alternative was possible. These provisions were in some ways weak and open to varying interpretations: for instance, a report could be dispensed with even if the sentencers had a custodial sentence in mind if in their opinion the circumstances of the case made it unnecessary to obtain one; and the factors to be weighed before ruling out a non-custodial sentence were broadly defined – seriousness of the offence, considerations of public protection, and the offender's ability and willingness to co-operate with a non-custodial penalty. All the same, by clarifying what sentencers should bear in mind, it provided an opening for social workers to construct arguments for non-custodial measures in their SIRs; and by introducing new conditions, like the 'specified activities' order, which could be incorporated into supervision orders, it increased the range of potentially diversionary options.

The 1988 Criminal Justice Act (the effects of which are not clear at the time of writing) tightens the criteria. While retaining the criterion of seriousness, it also specifies that a custodial sentence can only be imposed on a young person if the court is satisfied that the offence is such that a custodial sentence would be imposed on an adult; or that the offender has a history of failing to respond to non-custodial measures, as well as being at the present time unable or unwilling to do so; or that only a custodial sentence would protect the public from serious harm from the offender – that is, a custodial sentence cannot be justified on grounds of general deterrence, so there should be no room for exemplary sentences. The court must say which of these criteria applies, and explain this to the defendant in everyday language. The Act provides some ground for hope that the legal basis which now allows social workers to argue against custody for juveniles can be extended to young adults.

Following the 1982 Act, in 1983, the DHSS issued a circular, LAC/85(3), which announced that £15 million were to be made available for the development of IT programmes, with preference being given to schemes which could provide 'intensive' IT as an alternative to care or custody. It is fair to say that this announcement was greeted with something short of rejoicing among large sections of the IT community. There was some suspicion of the fact that the grants were to be made to voluntary organisations (this was more a means of by-passing the rate support grant than the product of a dogmatic conviction that voluntary organisations should be involved at the expense of the state sector). The anxiety was about how the money would be used: how could anyone be sure that it would go to projects that really could divert from custody? What was to prevent 'net-widening'? These fears seemed initially to be confirmed by the way the money was allocated in the first months of the scheme. It looked as if decisions might be made on a rather arbitrary basis: whichever voluntary organisations put in their bids first were liable to receive the grants, regardless of assessments of local need or demand. The circular did indeed provide a welcome opportunity for national child care organisations to move into a new area, as their traditional area of concern, residential care, became less viable. Thus in the early stages of the project it looked as if the South-West, for example, might be over-provided with resources, while areas with much higher levels of custodial sentencing, such as the industrial North-West, were under-provided. But these early anomalies were quite quickly corrected (partly because the DHSS officials realised that they did not need to worry that they would not be able to get rid of the money); and the subsequent careful monitoring of the initiative by NACRO's juvenile crime unit (NACRO, 1988) suggests that its effect overall has been to contribute to the marked reduction in custodial sentencing of juveniles which has occurred during the 1980s.

To what extent can social work agencies claim the credit for this decline in the use of custody (and the virtual disappearance in most areas of care orders in criminal proceedings)? The question cannot be answered exactly, though it is interesting that the Government seems to believe that the development of intensive IT schemes is at least partly responsible (Home Office, 1988c). Another major factor, however, is the demographic change which has meant that the number of juveniles in the population as a whole has declined quite rapidly since the mid-1970s. That is, the number eligible to be processed by the juvenile justice has decreased independently of the efforts of social workers or anyone else. Pratt (1985) wrote of delinquency as a 'scarce resource', pointing to the likelihood of a decline of over 25 % in the overall cohort between 1977 and 1991, and predicting a 'shortage of customers' for the courts and social work agencies. At around the same time, it started to become clear to the staff of a number of intensive IT schemes that they were dealing with far lower numbers of juveniles than had been envisaged when the centres were set up – and this was not only in areas where the number at risk of custody had always been too low to justify intensive provision.

Cautioning and diversion

In a sense, these centres were victims of the success of the system management strategies which, in line with the research and policy prescriptions outlined above, had developed through the 1980s as the corollary of face-to-face work with offenders. In particular (and this is not necessarily an achievement attributable to social work), the use of cautions had increased substantially, and was to continue to do so. Overall, the use of cautions, as a percentage of those found guilty, rose from 44 % for boys and 65 % for girls in 1971 to 66 % and 87 % respectively in 1987. The increase for boys, however, occurred entirely in the 1980s; the figure for 1980 was still only 44 %, and had not (despite official encouragement) shown any consistent upward trend in the 1970s. The 1980 White Paper explicitly endorsed the practice of cautioning as the method of preference for dealing with first offenders, but, as several commentators noted, practice continued to vary widely between police forces (Tutt and Giller, 1983; Laycock and Tarling, 1985). In 1984, the Home Office issued a consultative document which argued both that the overall use of cautions should be increased and that there should be greater consistency between areas, and this was followed by Circular 14/1985, which also encouraged increased inter-agency co-operation. This has not entirely removed discrepancies between areas (Giller and Tutt, 1987), but it does seem to have inspired some police forces at least to raise their cautioning rates. For example, Cumbria's rate increased from well below the national average in 1984 to well above it in 1987 (Smith and Blagg, 1989).

The highest rate of cautioning over the past few years has consistently been in Northamptonshire, an area which also has probably the most elaborate system of inter-agency consultation, in the form of juvenile bureaux which in effect act as independent diversion agencies (Centre of Youth, Crime and Comunity, 1984). It is tempting to conclude that, if the aim is diversion, inter-agency consultation is the answer; and indeed it is, as we have shown, very often treated as something not far short of a panacea for the ills of the criminal justice system. But some scepticism is in order. It is possible that Northamptonshire is something of a special case, with the police both keen to increase the cautioning rate and willing to share their decision-making power with other agencies. These conditions do not apply every-where. Laycock and Tarling (1985) suggested, in examining possible reasons for the variation in cautioning rates between areas, that the important factor was the policy of the police. Where this entailed a predisposition in favour of cautioning first offenders, but was flexible enough to allow others also to be cautioned, the overall rate tended to be high. The presence or absence of formal procedures for inter-agency co-operation did not appear to affect cautioning rates. It seems reasonable to conclude that if the police do not enter such inter-agency consultations with a policy that broadly favours diver-sion, it will be very difficult for other agencies to influence the out-come. For instance, the cautioning rate in Greater Manchester has remained comparatively low despite the considerable effort put into consultations with the police by social workers and probation offi-cers; and most of the increase in cautioning in Cumbria could be attributed to a change in the views of the police alone, rather than to the work of the multi-agency cautioning panels (Smith and Blagg, 1989).

Diversion from prosecution through an increase in cautioning is an aim which, as Pratt (1986) has noted, seems to command support right across the ideological spectrum. It is an aim which we entirely support, since (if achieved) it will reduce the numbers of young people who are stigmatised by a conviction and thus run the risk of becoming enmeshed in the criminal justice system. A few words of caution about cautioning seem necessary, however. Firstly, it is quite possible to increase the number of cautions in any area by drawing more juveniles into the system (widening the net) rather than by the use of cautioning as an alternative to prosecution (diversion). The early studies of cautioning suggested that it entailed at least as much net-widening as diversion (Ditchfield, 1976; Farrington and Ben-nett, 1981; Parker, Casburn and Turnbull, 1981), and this remains at least a theoretical possibility, although it seems unlikely as an explan-ation of the great increase in cautioning in the last few years. The police are after all often interested in cautioning as a means of saving time and effort and allowing them to concentrate resources on other, more pressing aspects of crime, and it would be self-defeating if cau-tioning generated more rather than less work.

Secondly, a preference for cautioning as opposed to prosecution entails the view that decisions which would otherwise be made by a court can and should be made by an executive agency – either the police alone or the police in liaison with other agencies. While no sys-tem of criminal justice can work without some executive discretion, a practice like that in Northampton, where repeated cautions are com-mon, does represent a substantial shift of power from courts to the juvenile bureaux, as the local magistrates, who are almost alone among the relevant parties in opposing the scheme, clearly recognise.

In other areas, such as Cumbria, where the existence of a 'reparation' scheme encouraged the 'enhancement' of cautions by some form of reparation, the potential problems of executive justice emerge still more clearly, since the panels sometimes ordered financial 'reparation' (on a very dubious legal basis) on a scale which probably exceeded anything a court would have considered appropriate by way of compensation.

You do not have to be a rigorous advocate of getting 'back to justice' to worry about such powers being exercised by a group which meets in secret, makes up its own rules as it goes along, decides cases in the absence of the offender, and allows no room for representation or appeal. Our own view is that social work agencies should be very clear about the aims and values which inform their participation in such informal tribunals if they are not be drawn into an extension of control in 'a new regulatory field over minor delinquency' (Pratt, 1986). The justification of inter-agency liaison over 'caution or prosecute' decisions is essentially a pragmatic one: it needs to be judged by its results. If it can be shown to work as a diversion from prosecution, without any tendency to substitute executive for judicial punishment, then its outcomes should be regarded as positive; and if not, not. If this pragmatic argument is accepted, with all that it entails by way of an increase in the power of executive agencies at the expense of the courts, it means that all attempts to use cautions as a means of reducing prosecutions need to be carefully and continuously monitored and evaluted. The monitoring guide produced by NACRO (Juvenile Crime Section, 1988) is useful in suggesting how this might be done, and encouraging in that it shows an awareness of the need for it.

The second way in which social work agencies may have contributed to the reduction in the use of custody is by developing programmes of work with juvenile offenders which appeal sufficiently to sentencers to encourage them to pass non-custodial sentences in cases where they would otherwise have passed custodial ones. In the nature of things the extent to which this has been achieved is hard to measure: how can you know when a supervision order has been made as an alternative to custody? The answer is that you cannot: measures of diversion from custody are necessarily indirect. But if you can show that (for example) juveniles attending an IT centre resemble in terms of number and seriousness of previous convictions those sentenced to custody elsewhere, and that the proportion of juveniles sentenced to custody in your local court has declined, then you can reasonably infer that your centre has had some effect. As we suggested in the previous chapter, Peter Raynor's (1988) evaluation of a probation centre in South Wales provides probably the most sophisticated example available of how this kind of evaluation might be carried out. There is as yet no comparable evaluation of a project for

juveniles, though several 'do-it-yourself' evaluations from within
projects, mostly not as well publicised as they should be, report
encouraging results (Children's Society Advisory Committee, 1988).

Social inquiry reports

Assuming that some success in diversion from custody may be
achieved, it will be based on two main elements. You need a form of
social work which sentencers know about, and are prepared to regard
as appropriate for cases which they might otherwise deal with by a
custodial sentence; and you need to be able to persuade them in particular cases that they ought to exercise this option. The second element of course logically precedes the first; and it is because the
importance of this has been recognised that there has been a great
deal of emphasis over the last few years on social inquiry reports
(SIRs), as the main means available to social work agencies of trying
to influence sentencing practice. This interest has not been confined
to juveniles, but in some ways the debates about SIRs have focused
on work in the juvenile rather than the adult courts – perhaps
because of a belief that had developed by the early 1980s (at least in
England and Wales) that it was important to do something, and that
it was possible to improve an aspect of social work practice that was
widely felt to be failing its clients. It was generally accepted both that
things were bad, and that they could be improved.

Social inquiry reports are both theoretically and practically important in that they represent the convergence of the two main areas of
social work practice which we have distinguished throughout: systems management and face-to-face work with offenders. Thus there
has been a good deal of interest in how SIRs can be used to keep
juveniles 'down tariff', by suggesting discharges, fines and attendance centre orders, for example, rather than supervision. Some commentators (Tutt and Giller, 1984) have argued that this is the main
way in which SIRs should be conceived, and this line of thinking is
reflected in the position of the Association for Juvenile Justice
described above, which is inherently suspicious of any claim that
social work might be helpful rather than harmfully stigmatising.
Many IT projects have also tried to develop this strategic approach to
SIR writing, following the basic principle of 'minimum intervention'. In some instances, such as the Community Alternatives for
Young Offenders project in Macclesfield, they have succeeded in
showing how easy and dangerous it is for social workers to assume
that sentencers will accept nothing short of drastic intervention in a
juvenile's life, when in fact, if the case is made clearly enough, they
may be persuaded to accept a low tariff option. Something like this
view of the uses of SIRs also appears in recent Home Office guidance
to the probation service (Home Office, 1984), in which it is made

clear that the provision of SIRs should be applied particularly to cases where there is a risk of custody, rather than to those in which there might be a need or wish for social work intervention.

This view of SIRs led Henri Giller to claim that they are 'not a social work document'. By this he means that they should not pathologise offenders by seeking dubious 'explanations' for their offence in their social or family history; and they should be aimed at achieving the 'least restrictive sanction' rather than at finding reasons for social work involvement. But, as Bottoms and Stelman (1988) point out, in their very useful analysis and practice guide on SIRs, this argument assumes that it is reasonable for the SIR writer to have in mind all the considerations that the court may want to weigh, instead of representing a distinctive (social work) perspective; and if followed in practice, there would be no difference between the SIR and the defence plea of mitigation. We agree with Bottoms and Stelman that the structural position of the SIR writer *vis-à-vis* the court means that he or she cannot take into account everything that the court may consider, and that it is important to retain a view of the SIR as distinctively a social work document, informed by social work values. Bottoms and Stelman list these as respect for persons, care for persons, and hope for the future and recognition of clients' potential for survival and growth (p 41); while in the nature of things there is always going to be room for argument about such lists, we think this one is useful, and provides a satisfactory support for other principles – for example, that social workers should never suggest custodial sentences.

The 1980s have seen renewed official and academic interest in SIRs as a social work task, which is a welcome development, as they had received little sustained attention since the highly influential Streatfield Report of 1961. In the early 1980s many practitioners began to question the value of traditional SIR practice, with its emphasis on family background and history, and to wonder what this had to do with offending. They were right to do so: much of the established practice of SIR writing rested on some variety of the 'treatment model', which we argued at the start of the previous chapter should be abandoned. This sort of questioning was soon echoed in policy-making circles, in local guidelines on SIRs, for example, and in a series of Home Office Circulars (two in 1983, one in 1986) which gave advice to the probation service on the content of SIRs and how sentencing suggestions should be presented. In 1987 rather similar guidelines for social workers appeared (DHSS, 1987). There are several common themes in these documents, two of which we want to highlight. They emphasise that the information contained in SIRs should be relevant to the reason why the report was being prepared – that is, to offending; and that the reasons for sentencing suggestions should be clearly and specifically set out. In particular, it is argued that it is not good enough to say that someone could benefit from a period of supervision; the reasons for thinking so also need to be set out, and an account given of what supervision would actually consist of. SIRs, then, were to focus more on offence – or offending, and suggestions for social work intervention were to be much more detailed and specific than had often been the case.

We can see in this conception of SIRs how they can be used as contractual documents, as suggested by Raynor (1985). The social work agency makes a commitment to provide a certain kind of service, and the defendant, on the basis of valid information, agrees to make use of the service, within certain specified constraints covering attendance, participation, and so on. The remaining question is: what should the service consist of? Increasingly, the answer for both juveniles and (belatedly and less certainly) adults is that it should entail a range of social work, usually but not necessarily groupwork, approaches which are appropriate to the problems which in the view of both worker and client are relevant to offending. As SIRs have focused more on offending, so has the associated social work practice. The advantages of such a specific, narrow focus are said to be those of relevance, credibility and (perhaps) effectiveness; critics complain of the use of social work for purposes of social control which supposedly results from making offending the core problem to be dealt with by social workers. We should like to review the arguments briefly here.

Offending-focused work

The principle that work with offenders should have something to do with offending is certainly not new, but the forms and practices of work which now characterise much IT practice in England and Wales can be traced to some fairly specific sources. Thorpe et al (1980) were, as we noted earlier, concerned both with system management issues and with direct work with juvenile offenders; they argued that work with the most serious and persistent offenders should be developed into what they called, perhaps unfortunately, a 'correctional curriculum'. The term seems unfortunate in that it suggests too confidently that the approach advocated will have correctional effects – that it will prevent or reduce further offending; and it sounds presumptuously scientific, as if a curriculum had actually been developed that would have this desired effect. In practice, what was advocated was fairly modest – a form of training in social skills using role play, rehearsal and video, which drew for its theoretical justification on the classic work of David Matza on the importance of the 'situation of company' in understanding juvenile delinquency (Matza, 1964). The practical suggestions were thus broadly in line with the social skills approach advocated by Philip Priestley and his colleagues, which, as we have seen, was becoming influential at the time in work with adult offenders (Priestley *et al*, 1977). The main difference was the emphasis of Thorpe and his colleagues on offence-focused work – not just any social skills, but those most directly related to offending in a delinquent group.

The correctional curriculum, however modest its actual scope, soon became influential in IT practce; one of its attractions, as with social skills work generally, may well have been that it gave social workers and their clients something to do rather than something to talk about. The same applies to the influential extension and development of the correctional curriculum idea by Gary Denman (1982), who also provided a slightly different and more elaborate theoretical justification for his practical proposals. In particular Denman drew on the work in cognitive psychology of Fishbein and Ajzen (1975) and their theory of reasoned action (TORA). Originally applied and empirically tested in such fields as voting behaviour and consumer choice, this theory sees all action as the product of two variables, beliefs and attitudes (for its application to crime, see Riley and Tuck, 1986). Discussing juvenile offending, Denman suggested that it was important to distinguish between the situationally specific beliefs and attitudes which might affect the reasoning of a youth contemplating, say, a burglary, and the more stable beliefs and attitudes which constituted, in Matza's phrase, the individual's 'philosophical inner life'. For example, a juvenile who strongly believed that the outcome of the burglary would be the acquisition of money and peer group status, and whose attitude towards this outcome was strongly positive, might nevertheless decide against it if he or she also believed that burglary was inherently wrong.

Denman provided a theoretical scheme which linked specific offending behaviour with 'background' factors – an individual's biography which had generated his or her stable (but not immovable) beliefs and attitudes. In this respect Denman succeeded where the traditional treatment model had failed: the main problem with this model for social workers was that it rarely provided a convincing account of just how the present offence was 'caused' by the defendant's childhood experiences, the presence of which in SIRs and other diagnoses was therefore inevitably free-floating and of doubtful relevance. Denman's cognitive approach made these connections intelligible and accessible, not only to workers but, potentially, to clients. He also did juvenile offenders the courtesy, entailed by the principle of respect for persons, of treating their offending as the product of some sort of process of reasoning (however truncated or logically flawed); and he took their philosophical inner life seriously.

More than this, he told social workers what to do (although we are sure that he would repudiate the 'painting by numbers' way his work has sometimes been used). Denman linked each level of reasoning with specific suggestions for social work assessment, providing a structure through which the juvenile's own account and interpretation of events could be elicited. He then showed how each level of assessment could lead on to group or individual work with a particular focus – for example, the immediate, situational reasoning that led to the offence could be role-played and reinterpreted in much the same way as that suggested by Thorpe and his colleagues; and the more stable beliefs and attitudes could be discussed, explored, and fed back to the client for review and criticism. Denman's scheme also allowed space for family work, which IT practitioners are often accused of neglecting, since it enabled links to be made between juveniles' beliefs about offending, authority and the law and their developmental experiences.

Denman's influential work in our view deserves the acclaim which it has received among practitioners. In various forms, including the computer programs it inspired, it is almost certainly the most widely used model of practice in present-day 'intensive' IT, and is increasingly influential in the probation service. Among much else, it is the clearest example known to us of the constructive use of a psychological theory in social work practice, and (unlike some narrowly behavioural approaches) it is thoroughly compatible with what we take to be the core values of social work. Nevertheless (and of course) its influence has been criticised: Denman himself has reservations about its more mechanistic applications, including the use of computers. Some of these criticisms, however, seem simply unjustified. For example, Pitts (1988), writing of the 'correctional curriculum' in general but inevitably, given its wide influence, with Denman's work somewhere in mind, complains of the 'politically timely emergence of a revitalised Pavlovian behaviourism' (p 113). We know of no IT centre in which Pavlovian behaviourism is practised; if one exists, it is certainly not using Denman's model. The latter draws on cognitive rather than behavioural psychology, and only counts as behaviourism if the term is extended to include thoughts and feelings (behaviour in the head), or if behaviourism is the label attached to everything which is not clearly psychodynamic in origin. If the alternative to cognitive psychology as an approach to understanding offending is the old treatment model, with its view of offending as the eruption from the unconscious of compulsive Oedipal drives, then we know which we prefer.

Another alternative is a more sociological approach, which has generated criticisms which we find more convincing. Pitts (1988) rehearses some of these. The essential argument is that in narrowing and concentrating its focus on high-risk offenders the 'new orthodoxy' in IT neglects issues of structural inequality and social need; delinquency becomes a problem of technical management, and the wider problems of discrimination and oppression – on the basis of class, race or gender – are ignored. There are clearly important issues here, and, as we hope to have made clear in earlier chapters, we think they need to be taken seriously by all those concerned with providing services for young people. For example, NACRO's monitoring of the 1983 DHSS initiative suggests that young black people are under-represented in intensive IT projects (and they seem to be overrepresented in custody); and Hudson (1988) convincingly criticises much IT practice for its masculinist assumptions.

It is of course true that if all social workers and allied professionals did about juvenile offending was to run intensive IT programmes as alternatives to custody they would be failing to respond adequately to the present problems of vulnerable youth; but this is not all they are doing, and to criticise the emphasis of much current IT practice for its selectivity and focus is in our view misleading. It seems highly likely that the development of offence-focused groupwork, combined with a sensitive and well-informed strategic approach to the juvenile justice system, has contributed substantially to the reduction of the use of custody in many areas. It would be odd for advocates of a better deal for vulnerable young people to complain about this; and while we too have reservations about some currently influential views, such as the narrowly technical concern with system management which sometimes appears in work associated with the Association for Juvenile Justice (AJJ), it is insulting to many practitioners in intensive IT projects to suppose that they are blithely unaware of the relevance of wider economic, cultural and social pressures to the problems of the juveniles with whom they work. If our interpretation of the findings of research is correct, there is no reason for the defensive, 'holding the line' stance which does undoubtedly characterise some practice in IT; as the work of the AJJ itself shows, a serious attempt to reduce the local use of custody is quite compatible with an active involvement in campaigning for social reform or legislative change – and with a commitment to anti-racist and anti-sexist practice.

Conclusions – social work and punishment

We want now to draw together some of the issues which have emerged in these two chapters. This is a task which we feel has an unusual political urgency about it at the time of writing, because the Government is in the process (perhaps) of evaluating its proposals for 'punishment in the community' in the light of the various comments on the 1988 Green Paper; and the Home Office is certainly awaiting with interest the responses of the local probation areas to its 'Action Plan'. As we noted towards the end of the previous chapter, the

Government is keen that the probation service, in conjunction with other agencies, should apply to work with young adult offenders the policies and practices which have had some apparent success with juveniles. Many of these have originated with voluntary organisations working in partnership with local authorities, in projects established with LAC 83(3) money or through NACRO's work in fostering inter-agency co-ordination. It is not surprising, then, that the responses to the Green Paper and the Action Plan by such organisations as NACRO, the Children's Society and the AJJ have been broadly favourable; it was hardly necessary for the AJJ (1989) to advise the Government to heed the lessons from work with juveniles in its consideration of young adult offenders, since the Government was making it clear that this was exactly what it was doing.

Surprisingly perhaps, by comparison with these responses NAPO's submission (NAPO, 1988) is a good deal less favourable. NAPO, for example, disagrees with the suggestion that the courts should be kept informed of the progress of offenders subjected to some form of intensive supervision as an alternative to custody, which by contrast NACRO regards as an essential element of a comprehensive local strategy to reduce custody. NAPO is also suspicious of the involvement of voluntary organisations in statutory supervision, which is now commonplace in work with juveniles, and which NACRO would again regard as an important aspect of inter-agency co-ordination. This suspicion can produce resistance to specific partnership-type proposals – there is a vivid account of one local branch's response to a management proposal (made before the Green Paper) to establish a joint project with the Rainer Foundation in a recent issue of the *Probation Journal* (Greater Manchester NAPO, 1988). Some of NAPO's concerns are perhaps inevitable and understandable given its status as a Trades Union as well as a professional association – concerns about dilution through the introduction of untrained staff, and about resources which could be allocated to the service going instead to voluntary organisations. Others, however, relate to the substantive proposals; and here there is more common ground than NAPO may realise with the views of the relevant voluntary organisations – but within a different overall perspective.

What mainly differentiates NAPO's overall view from that of the organisations with experience in developing intensive non-custodial measures for juveniles is its pessimism. As we noted when summarising the relevant provisions of the 1988 Criminal Justice Act, there are some grounds for optimism about the feasibility of applying to young adults the same criteria for custody as have been applied to juveniles. But instead of emphasising the similarities between work with juveniles and young adults NAPO emphasises the differences. Thus it is argued (NAPO, 1988, p 17) that young adults will often have previous convictions, sometimes for more serious offences, that 'because of their adult appearance many are less likely to attract a sympathetic response', that the behaviour of young adults is the object of particular social concern and that they are 'therefore likely to be treated more severely', and that the fact that many are sentenced in the Crown Court creates a special difficulty, since it is likely to be difficult to involve judges in an inter-agency strategy. All this means that it is likely to be more difficult to reduce the use of custody for young adults than for juveniles; 'but nevertheless an opportunity may exist to make some progress'.

While some of these points may seem a bit weak, it is quite true that custody for young adults will be a hard nut to crack: they are not just likely to be treated more severely than juveniles, they *are* treated more severely. Nevertheless, the difficulties involved in reducing the use of custody for juveniles were (and are) real: it is easy to forget that the rate of custodial sentences for juveniles had increased much more rapidly than for young adults during the 1970s. There was a strong tide that had to be turned; but, on the whole, it has been turned. NAPO's pessimism contrasts sharply with the optimism of the voluntary organisations, and it is hard to see what justifies it as a penological prediction, let alone a negotiating tactic. Nothing could be better calculated to reassure the Government that it is on the right lines in contemplating the involvement of the voluntary sector in the supervision of young adults than the apparent gloom of the probation service about what it can do, compared with the buoyancy of the voluntary organisations about what they can do.

NAPO fears, among other things, that the voluntary organisations will be used as a stalking-horse for private enterprise. But, as we noted above, there is no real evidence that this has occurred in work with juveniles. It is, however, about to occur (not through the fault of the voluntary sector) with the experimental introduction of electronic tagging in the summer of 1989. NAPO's opposition to this is echoed in all the other submissions on the Green Paper we have seen: an opposition based not only on the element of privatisation but on a principled rejection of the idea of tagging – of civil liberties, of the extension of official control, of the uncertainty (to say the least) that it will actually be used only for those who would otherwise be in custody, of practical feasibility – together amount to a strong case against the introduction of tagging, though not one the Government is at present disposed to heed. The rejection of tagging is common ground between NAPO and the organisations it regards with such suspicion.

So is much else. There is a common rejection of the elements in the Government's proposals which are purely punitive and disciplinary. For example, the proposed 'supervision and restriction order' includes provision for something like house arrest and for a curfew, ideas which are reminiscent of some discredited (one had hoped) and unused parts of the 1982 Act. The curfew provision in that Act has remained largely a dead letter because of a widely shared view that it would be unenforceable – a view shared by the police. More than this, it is as clear to the voluntary organisations as to NAPO that such restrictions on liberty, whose purpose is purely punishment or control, unconnected with any attempt to provide social work help or support, are incompatible with the values which inherently inform social work practice. The Government itself may recognise this: the Green Paper suggests that the proposed new order might require a new agency to be set up for its enforcement, since the punitive elements might not be compatible with the values of the probation service. Indeed they would not be; nor would they be compatible with the values of, say, NCH. It is noteworthy, and sometimes not as clear as it should be, that some leading figures in the voluntary sector, including Gary Denman, have strongly opposed not only these parts of the Green Paper but also any further development of tracking.

Our own hope is that the proposals for a supervision and restriction order will be abandoned; or, if legislated for, not implemented. But it remains important to decide what other aspects of the Government's proposals are compatible with social work conceived as helping, and which are not. The Action Plan, describing what it is to be regarded as 'best practice' and exploring ideas for 'intensive probation', makes many suggestions which we think are constructive and point towards a possible way forward for the supervision of young adults. In fact, they are very largely founded on existing practice. The document emphasises the need for innovative measures to 'target' those most at risk of custody (showing an awareness of the 'net-widening' problem); for specificity and clarity in the presentation of non-custodial options to courts; for the content of supervision to include work on offending behaviour as well as on specific problems such as drug or alcohol abuse and illiteracy; and for the programmes to be rigorously monitored and evaluated. All of this, it seems to us, is or should be common ground.

In some respects, the Action Plan is quite a radical text: it suggests, for example, that 'alternatives to custody' is 'an expression which should be avoided, with its implication that custody is somehow the standard or normal disposal'. A very few years ago, this idea seemed excitingly radical and challenging when we encountered it at IT and similar conferences. Among other things, the Action Plan shows signs of such critical influences; it may be disconcerting to researchers and practitioners who sometimes feel that nobody is listening to discover that someone in the Home Office was. But – and the qualification is important – there are other proposals which betray a failure to distinguish between aspects of supervision which are compatible with helping and those which are not. For instance, the idea that a probation order might include the client's commitment to frequent reporting for a period of a few weeks does not in principle or practice (since it is already quite common) conflict with the values and aims of social work; it depends on what happens when the client frequently reports, and on whether he or she understood and accepted the reasons for the frequency of reporting. On the other hand, the proposal slipped unobtrusively into the discussion of 'intensive probation' – that there might be a requirement to report at 'unsocial hours' – does seem to us to conflict in a potentially damaging way with the aim of helping the client, since the requirement can only be designed to be deliberately irksome and punitive.

Our view is that it is only by getting such distinctions clear that social work agencies can avoid the two most worrying possibilities that the Government's proposals raise. The first is the familiar one that social work with offenders will become indistinguishable from repression, surveillance and control. A clear and (as far as possible) consistent view of what the talk of social work aims and values means for practice is the best defence against this – and one which has already been fairly successful, for example in heading off proposals for curfews and preventive arrests, as envisaged in the Younger Report. The second, less familiar possibility is that social work will come to be defined as irrelevant in the new agenda of punishment in the community. This would be bad for the social work agencies and disastrous for their erstwhile clients. The best defence seems likely to be a cautious optimism, and we think that the experience of the reduction of custody for juveniles does justify such a position. Certainly there are differences between the juvenile and adult systems, but they are still the same kind of system. It is demonstrable that work with juveniles has developed under the broad banner of intensive IT which has won some credibility with sentencers without losing a sense of social work values, and there is no reason why a similar approach with young adults should not hold out some prospect of similar success. This will entail some enhancement or strengthening of probation orders in appropriate cases, but this is nothing new; it is odd that a service which has been running probation hostels for many years should baulk at the prospect of orders being enhanced by far less restrictive conditions.

Raynor (1985) sets out very clearly the principles and criteria which can inform and justify the enhancement of probation. He suggests that the important general principles which should inform social work's attempts to influence the criminal justice system are: maximum feasible voluntarism, maximum feasible participation, recognition of responsibility, social justice (personal responsibility is not all that should be considered), creativity (in providing services), and effectiveness. Forms of enhanced probation, he suggests, should meet the following criteria:

1. They should be significantly less coercive than the custody they are intended to replace.

2. They should be offered only on the basis of the client's fully informed consent rather than on a 'take it or leave it' basis.

3. Programmes should be flexible enough to allow some negotiation and client choice about how demands should be met, rather than totally pre-determined.

4. Both induction into a programme and its continuing implementation should include substantial opportunities for probationers to explore problems, assess their situation, consider realistic possibilities of help relating to agreed difficulties, and enter into negotiated commitments of this kind if they wish (pp 187–8).

We could add (by way of expanding the implications of the third point) that there should be room for the exercise of reasonable discretion on what action (if any) to take if the client breaches the order. Without this the conditions are likely to be perceived by both parties as merely and mechanically restrictive; and the more conditions there are, the higher the breach rate will inevitably be. Extra conditions intended to enhance the order should be kept to a minimum; the proliferation of restrictive clauses threatened by the Green Paper should be (and is being) resisted.

Raynor's statement is a useful starting point for thinking about how to respond to the new demands of the Green Paper and the Action Plan, and from contacts with practitioners and managers in probation and other agencies we think that Raynor's principles command a good deal of support. There will always be room for argument (about social work involvement in reparation schemes, for instance), but we also believe that there is more of a consensus among informed practitioners than the often noisy polemics tend to suggest.

We have concentrated here on a particular and pressing debate. This focus should not detract from our continuing commitment, expressed in earlier chapters, to a broad and open conception of how social workers, in conjunction with other professional groups, can try to improve the conditions of life for young people in trouble, for those enmeshed in the criminal justice system, and for those affected by crime and the unhappiness associated with it. This may sound grandiose, but we prefer a (cautious) optimism to a defensive, anxious pessimism: a rational preference, because optimism makes for better social work. The innovations and developments we have described – in social crime prevention, in victim–offender mediation, in community involvement – have not been uniformly successful, but they represent the vitality of the social work tradition of optimistic humanism. In the dark visions of Stanley Cohen (1985) and in related writings, there is an abundance of pessimism of the intelligence; as Cohen, to his credit, recognises, we also need optimism of the will, and this may be the distinctive quality social work can bring to debates on crime and criminal justice. We hope to have shown that optimism needs no apology.

7 Reparation, mediation and juvenile crime: philosophy and practice

In recent years there have been a number of experiments which have explored the potential of incorporating an element of reparation and mediation into the criminal justice system. Much of this work has been initiated by probation officers and social workers anxious, perhaps, to find a new role in the 'post-treatment' epoch. Many professionals have also become actively involved with the issue because they have felt that the interests and needs of victims have never been adequately catered for in a system which has tended to focus almost exclusively on the offender (Harding, 1987; Smith *et al*, 1988). Many probation officers with whom we have come into contact have, for example, moved into the reparation/mediation area having gained valuable experience working as volunteers for the National Association of Victim Support Schemes.

The debate about reparation has been influenced by the current concern about the increasing complexity of the criminal justice system, especially the mysteries of the tariff as the basis for imposing sanctions upon offenders. Reparation offers a means of making the 'punishment fit the crime': offenders would, presumably, understand better the meaning of a sanction incorporating reparation, while victims would reap the benefit of seeing the injury inflicted upon them dealt with on its own terms, rather than according to obscure criteria unrelated to the offence. Reparation promises to harmonise aims often thought to be conflicting and incompatible, both humanising the system and retaining society's duty to punish miscreants; justice could finally be combined with welfare. This belief is reinforced by a commonsense appeal to social ideals of 'natural justice', which tend to favour disposals on the eye-for-an-eye principle. It seems, on the face of it, eminently reasonable to provide offence resolutions which put the interests of victims first and direct any restitution towards them.

On the whole, though, much of what takes place in the name of reparation is still concentrated upon the offender, which is hardly surprising given that so much of the work takes place within a context mapped out by the criminal justice system, or at least in its shadow. Victims have little opportunity themselves to instigate any process of reparation, other than informally – which some of course do, particularly in small communities where the victim and offender may be linked by relationships that precede the offence. The fact remains that the majority of victims who become involved in reparation in the system are, in a sense, 'recruited' to a process which is aimed at providing a form of punishment or a learning experience for offenders – even the payment of compensation to victims, or a formal apology, can be construed as a form of punishment for offenders: its severity as a sanction intensified rather than diminished because it takes place, so to speak, 'at the scene of the crime'. Here one can certainly find echoes of Foucault's thesis that self-styled 'reforms' come about not to punish less but to punish more, to punish deeper (Foucault, 1977; Cohen, 1985). Not all victims find this unjust (see below), but many end up feeling that the spectacle has been put on for the offender's benefit rather than for theirs (see Davis *et al*, 1988). Before moving on to discuss particular schemes in detail it is necessary to chart briefly the emergence of the reparation/mediation movement.

The critique

Few developments in the criminal justice system can have captured both official and popular imagination to quite the same extent and with quite the same rapidity as the sudden advocacy for victim/offender mediation. This dramatic eruption of interest was matched by the virtual unanimity of support for the idea voiced by widely differing professional, voluntary and political bodies. Certainly, there was little anyone could object to in the principle of reparation and mediation, although the forms it was to take could worry many observers, and still do. One reason for its appeal was that it crystallised a range of concerns: concerns about redressing the grievances of victims, as we have already suggested, but also concerns about the criminal justice system itself as an adequate vehicle for resolving conflicts between people. The movement for reparation gained some of its most compelling ideas from the works of people like Christie and Hulsman, who had argued (and here they reflected the philosophies of the 'small society' theorists) that the criminal justice system was too distant from the realities of everyday life; the best it could do was to 'steal' people's conflicts and prevent them from putting things right themselves (Christie, 1977; Hulsman, 1977). In the United States the idea has been strongly supported by a renascent Christian movement, largely Mennonite and Quaker in origin, emphasising the values of reconciliation and forgiveness as justifiable ends in themselves (Zehr, 1985; Marshall, 1984). The main emphasis in this notion of mediation is on informality, voluntariness, and negotiation; these principles, however, find it difficult to take root in the criminal justice system.

In this country these more esoteric concerns have, perhaps, been less important in shifting opinion in favour of change than the recognition that the existing system was failing (Wright, 1982) and so for that matter were attempts to reform it (Cohen, 1985). Those who shared Wright's enthusiasm for 'making good' as a possible alternative to the utilitarian aims which the established system had failed to achieve, were further heartened by the success of the growing movement for support of victims in largely 'depoliticising' an issue which had hitherto seemed to work entirely to the benefit of the authoritarian right; and by the evidence from a number of surveys of victims (Maguire, 1982; Shapland, 1984; Hough and Moxon, 1985) that victims were not as punitively inclined as had been widely supposed, and that many of them were interested both in reparation and in being more involved in the process of responding to a criminal act. The popularity of community service both with sentencers and (apparently) with offenders (Pease and McWilliams, 1981) is another likely influence, since community service could be conceived as 'indirect reparation'. The idea had a broad enough appeal to unite (presumably not all for the same reasons) the Home Secretary of the day (Brittan, 1984), the Labour Campaign for Criminal Justice (Downes, 1983), and the 'new realist' left-wing criminologists (Lea and Young, 1984).

The Home Office itself declared its interest by announcing in 1985 funding for four experimental projects, all but one originating in the probation service. Three of these schemes – in Coventry, Leeds and Wolverhampton – were 'court-based': that is, the attempt to bring victims and offenders together was made in the context of a forthcoming court appearance (see Figure 7.1). The fourth, in Cumbria, was 'police-based': here the attempt was normally made when it had already been decided that the offender should be cautioned. (For an evaluation of these projects see Marshall and Merry, 1989.) Although variations within these two broad categories of scheme are theoretically possible, and are found in practice, the distinction drawn by Marshall and Walpole (1985) – 'court-based' as against 'police-based' – is useful in indicating the two main points within the criminal justice process at which some form of mediation may take place. Police-based schemes will usually deal exclusively with juvenile offenders, since cautioning of adults, while legally possible, is rare in most police force areas (Laycock and Tarling, 1985); court-based schemes can deal with either, but in practice have concentrated on

Figure 7.1 Models of reparation/mediation: 'court-based'

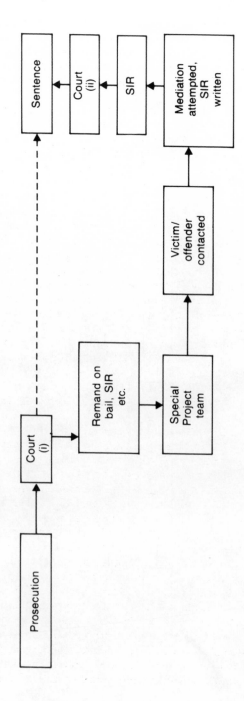

Figure 7.2 'Police based' Model 1: therapeutic/educational

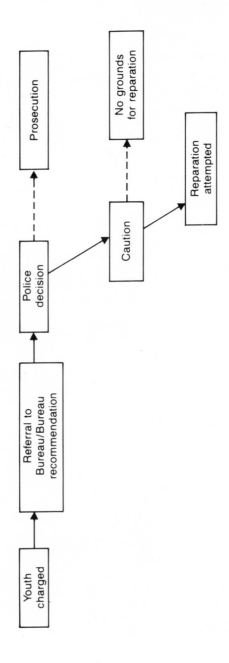

adults. There are at least two possible models of a 'police-based' scheme, described below in terms of their aims an procedures.

Model 1: Therapeutic/educational (diversion irrelevant)

In this variant, the decision about whether the victim and offender should be offered an opportunity to meet is taken independently of the decision to caution or prosecute; indeed it usually takes place post-caution. The ground for offering this opportunity is normally that some benefit can be expected to result for one or both parties. For example, the victim might welcome some tangible reparation, or the offender might gain an educative insight into the experience of victimisation (see Figure 7.2).

Model 2: Diversion 'on condition'

There are two variants of this: in the first, a caution is given on the understanding that the bare caution will be 'enhanced' by an attempt to bring the victim and offender together, or to get the offender to make some reparation. Although the caution is not made conditional on the offender's agreement to co-operate, the fact that the caution is linked in this way to an attempt at reparation may make it difficult for offenders to refuse. The attempt at reparation in this context is closely linked to the aim of diversion from prosecution; the driving force is a concern with the interests of offenders rather than of victims. In the second, the caution is made directly conditional upon the offender's agreement to, and perhaps completion of, some form of reparation. The decision to caution or prosecute may be deferred until the offender's response is known. Clearly in such cases the offender will be under considerable pressure to agree with the suggestion of reparation; less obviously, the victim too may be under pressure, if he or she knows that the result of a refusal to agree will be that a juvenile is prosecuted rather than cautioned (see Figure 7.3).

This element of coercion – which was present on occasion in the Cumbrian project (see below) – is paradoxical since one of the main sources of the initial interest in reparation was criticism of the coercive nature of the criminal justice system and its lack of scope for negotiated settlements (Christie, 1977; Raynor, 1985).

There is diversity, therefore, in the way reparation and mediation are employed within the criminal justice system. Moreover, there are differences in style between different schemes, with some attempting to bring about a genuine reconciliation between victim and offender via 'mediation', and others acting as debt enforcement agencies without the two parties necessarily becoming involved in an exchange of views, if, indeed, they are brought together at all. Our material for this chapter is derived mainly from the experience we have gained in

Figure 7.3   'Police-based' Model 2: Conditional

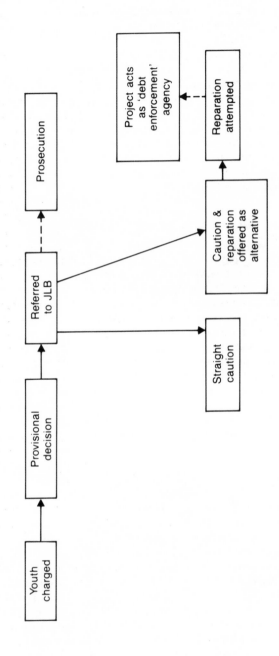

research carried out in various schemes, each with a different focus. The first was in Corby, Northamptonshire, which was the site of an innovatory juvenile liaison bureau staffed by full-time seconded representatives from the police, social services, probation, youth services and education; the second was a scheme funded by the Home Office in Cumbria, one of the four projects which were centrally funded on an experimental basis. This scheme, though run by the probation service, took its referrals from four juvenile panels run by the police with support from the social services (IT), education and probation, (for an evaluation of court-based schemes see Smith *et al*, 1988). Firstly we need to define reparation and mediation: thus far we have used the terms interchangeably, although they actually refer to two discrete processes.

Reparation

'Reparation' means, or should mean, some attempt by the offender to make amends for the harm done to the victim by the offence (cf. Davis *et al*, 1988). This might take various forms: financial compensation, material restitution, or work for the victim. Reparation need not require the offender's consent: the idea does not entail any implication of voluntariness; and it is compatible with an interest in retribution, as in the well-established case of compensation orders. In practice very different activities are often counted as reparation – on the one hand, for instance, the payment of compensation to the actual victim, and on the other, community service, in which reparation is conceived as being made 'indirectly' to the victimised 'community', or to the victims of other crimes, where an effort has been made to link community service with victim support.

Mediation

'Mediation' refers quite clearly to a process, not to an outcome; and it is perhaps unfortunate that some projects have come to be known as 'mediation' projects, as if this in itself made it clear that their aims were not confined to reparation (Smith *et al*, 1988). Mediation entails the intervention of a third party in a dispute, and is potentially useful only if the aim is to reach a more or less voluntary agreement between the parties as to how the dispute may be resolved. The process of mediation may take various forms: for instance, bringing the parties together or acting as a 'go-between'. It is not an inherent requirement that the parties should meet; the process might be conducted by letter. Most projects have, however, emphasised the importance of face-to-face meetings between victims and offenders.

Case study I - Northamptonshire: Corby

In this scheme, which approximated Model 1 of our typology (Figure 7.2), the decision about whether the victim and the offender should be offered an opportunity to meet is taken independently of the decision to caution or prosecute the offender. The bureaux in Northamptonshire had been generally successful in raising the cautioning rate by negotiation with the police and other agencies. In Corby, therefore, there was not a pressing need to 'offer' reparation to a sceptical police force as the price for increasing the use of cautioning. It could be employed not as a strategy to increase cautioning but as a more general attempt to improve services to victims as well as to provide an educational experience for offenders (as we shall see, there is cynicism in some quarters about the meaning for offenders of forms of reparation used to 'buy' a caution or a lighter sentence in court).

In the period November 1981 to November 1982, the Juvenile Bureau had 492 referrals, 77 of whom, according to the Bureau's figures, had taken part in some kind of offence resolution. Of this group 21 made direct reparation to the victim - that is, met the victim and compensated him/her in some way; 27 made an apology directly to the victim but did not pay compensation and 38 made reparation indirectly via some kind of community task or work. Seventeen of the young people were interviewed (2 girls and 15 boys) had participated in at least one of these forms of offence resolution; 14 had done indirect reparation, such as painting and repairs, not always for the victim, and work with the elderly; 11 had compensated the victim in some way, and 7 had made a direct apology to the victim.

Reparation was to be used selectively and only when a number of criteria had been met. Firstly, was the offence admitted? Was it an offence that could be resolved? Was the offender willing to participate? Was the proposed form of reparation appropriate, that is, in keeping with the scale of the offence? Did the victim agree to the idea and feel comfortable with the proposals? A policy statement illustrates the Bureau's aims:

> Hopefully offenders will come away from the experiences with a fuller understanding of the implications of their behaviour and an enhanced sense of responsibility towards the victim, and perhaps the wider community.
>
> We recognize this sort of resolution must be handled with care and sensitivity. Victims cannot be forced into facing offenders simply to fit 'tidy prescriptions', nor can offenders be compelled to make amends or to 'overcompensate' for an action (Hinks and Smith, 1985).

In interviews with the Bureau staff, it became clear that they were aware of the possible dangers inherent in reparation. They would never, they said, 'buy' a caution for a juvenile by offering reparation to the police, nor in fact use it in any way that could be considered punitive; rather they wished to use reparation as a means of resolving hurtful and problematic events in an undramatic way.

Offenders were asked to relate their experiences of reparation, to discover if it had an impact on them of the kind desired by the Bureau. What was it like to meet the victim of their criminal act? Had they learned anything from it? Had it made them feel differently about offending? Did they feel it was a form of punishment? Had they felt coerced into doing it?

One quickly recognised that there was no such thing as a straight-forward reparation. They all tended to leave the children 'feeling' different, often as a result of some quite complex factors, to do with feelings of natural justice, violated status, degree of felt guilt, community reaction, and so on. A direct apology to a victim, for example could be qualitatively different depending upon the type of offence, and the status of the actors involved. It led one to recognise that reparation touches not only upon issues of justice in the abstract, but becomes enmeshed with quite immediate issues of right and wrong. Certain kinds of reparative work fitted in perfectly with the children's own sense of fairness and natural justice; others did not.

It was useful, therefore, to distinguish between different types of reparation as each touched off very different reactions. The first category, institutional reparation, occurs when a youth is required to apologise (or in some other way make amends) to a representative of some organisation such as a shop or business. The second, personal reparation, occurs when reparation is made directly to another individual. There are very marked discrepancies of attitudes and experiences between the two models.

Reparation to institutions

This option seemed to be the least meaningful for the parties concerned in the process, particulary for the youth. In this case the 'victim' as such was not an individual but an organisation. Two cases can be used to illustrate this category. In one instance the shop manager and the youth were known to one another, which made the youth certain that the manager felt hostile towards him anyway, having frequently sent him out of the store; and in the other a boy was given a very public dressing-down by an irate manager of a large business, following a break-in.

Here the youths easily consigned the encounters to the traditional interaction with authority; both made comparisons with 'teachers'. Nothing new was required of them and the event became easily absorbed into the traditional narrative of working-class youth and authority.

Institutional reparation offers restricted scope for reconciliation and understanding. The interaction can be understood not as an alternative to the legal model but quite frequently as its reproduction in a less formal setting. The shopkeeper now takes on the role of the law, demanding apologies rather than a sentence. This is more the case because the manager will himself be acting as a representative of an institution and not a victim with a range of confused personal feelings and hurt emotions to sort out. It turns out that the offender and the manager find it difficult to escape the imperatives of their real positions. The result can well be a 'waste of time', at least for the young person. The Bureau workers felt uneasy about such encounters and increasingly used this option only in cases where the manager was particularly sensitive to the issues involved and where the young person was well prepared beforehand.

Situations weighted too far in the direction of the adult's need to admonish youthful misbehaviour, without there being any real opportunity for the youth himself to gain from the experience, were frequently regarded as unsuitable for reparation. The Bureau team became increasingly aware of the sensitive nature of the interaction they were establishing through reparation and were careful, after some initial difficulties in the early days, to avoid setting up situations in which the reparee felt humiliated or 'put on trial'. The Bureau policy was based upon the premise that, once a child had been cautioned, it was unfair then to exact retribution by some other, more insidious route. This could be the likely outcome of certain kinds of reparation where compensation is impractical or if the interaction is particularly humiliating.

Increasingly the Bureau tried to identify a 'victim' within an organisation, rather than someone remote from the incident. Two cases provide useful examples of this strategy. The first involved two boys who ran amok in a dairy and did considerable damage; here the Bureau arranged a meeting with the maintenance man who had been very distressed by the damage to 'his' place of work. In the second three boys broke windows and other property in their school; here the Bureau arranged for them to spend time with the janitor who had been responsible for clearing up the debris. In both instances there ws a clear sense of *personal* loss, even though these crimes could have been constructed as offences against institutions. In the second of our two models of institutional reparation the victim did suffer some personal damage or loss as a result of the offence. Interviews conducted with children who had undergone this process produced rather different accounts from those cited earlier. What one observed in such cases was a situation in which the relatively fixed, almost institutionalised responses of child and adult were transformed by the emergence of a new range of requirements from the interaction, primarily the need of the victim to have his or her anxiety and sense of threat removed and the desire of the offender to put something right. This need can open the way for the emergence of a wholly different kind of encounter as we shall attempt to illustrate.

As we have already suggested, there is a tendency within the criminal justice system for the original conflict to become detached, 'stolen' (Christie, 1977, p 4), and alienated from the immediate relationship of the victim and the offender. This has as one of its costs the almost total alienation of the victim and the offender from the process. More than this, it may tend to reinforce for the victim the more hurtful aspects of the offence. The judicial and social processes of criminal prosecution, especially in periods of moral panic about youth, may well have the effect of amplifying the victim's sense of threat and insecurity. The offender will appear in an even more devilish light than hitherto, having now entered the galley of folk devils.

For the offender the reality of the offence becomes submerged under the weight of the judicial process itself. It will also become buried somewhere back in time given the slowness of the process. 'Arrest' in this sense involves more than just a physical restriction of freedom; what is also 'arrested' is the capacity to right the wrong, as that power no longer resides with the original actors. Personal reparation raises the possibility of redressing grievances by permitting the original actors to put things right in a practical and undramatic manner. The 'demythologisation' of the offender may serve to drain some of the anxiety out of the incident for the victim and in turn provides a new series of expectations for the young offender, giving him/her an immediate and practical means of righting the wrong.

Personal reparation

Personal reparation is not always a straightforward process. Many of the cases examined were more complex and difficult. It became clear, for example, that the situation altered dramatically when the parties were known to one another and when there had been any history of conflict.

Juvenile offences often occur as but one step in a protracted series of encounters, often under peer-group pressure, as Blagg has suggested:

> This is particularly so in cases of fights between school-children, the incident occurring only after 'information' is passed between the actors by various interested go-betweens, who act as sources of information and fix up the event rather like matchmakers in rural communities. The resulting conflict often takes place on a confused set of grounds and reasons; victims, offenders and bystanders all may carry some responsibility (Blagg, 1985, p 256).

The problems created by peer-group and local knowledge, especially when status is threatened, were a consistent feature in the study and influenced the significance which reparation had for the child. In such cases the Bureau had to make certain that the child was making amends only for the part of the particular incident that had a criminal dimension. In one case for example, a boy damaged the door and window of a neighbour. He was charged for this and wanted to make amends for the damage. The offence, however, had taken place during a disagreement with the neighbour's son: it would have destroyed the boy's status locally had he been seen to be making amends to the other boy through the reparation. The case had to be handled sensitively so that the neighbour's child could not claim to have gained a victory over his adversary; the 'offender' sent a letter apologising for the damage and paid for the repair, rather than actually going round in person – this might have created a humiliating spectacle, punitive out of all proportion with the scale of the offence.

Case study II – The Cumbria Project

As suggested above, the Cumbrian scheme in practice contained elements of the second model of police-based reparation (see above). After the initial period of the project the workers tried to avoid working in a context in which a caution depended on the offender's response to the suggestion of reparation, but they did not always succeed. In other cases the offender (and/or the victim) believed that a caution depended on his or her agreement to reparation when this was not in fact so; it could be seen then as being implicitly coercive. The pattern is predictable since the main justification for the scheme, as set out in the original proposal to the Home Office from the local probation service, was that reparation might promote the aim of diversion from prosecution. This was a live issue in the area since the police had recently taken the initiative in setting up juvenile liaison panels in each of the four police divisions, based in Barrow (South), Kendal (East), Carlisle (North) and Whitehaven/Workington (West). The panels met fortnightly to consider cases which in the view of the police were suitable for discussion – neither self-evident cautions nor inescapable prosecutions. The meetings were chaired by a chief inspector from the local division, and attended by the police juvenile liaison officer, who acted as secretary, the local probation officer with responsibility for juveniles, the divisional intermediate treatment officer, representing the social services department, and an education welfare officer.

Despite the establishment of the panels, it was not generally thought, by the police representatives or anyone else, that there was a clear commitment on the part of the police to increase the cautioning rate at the expense of prosecutions. In Cumbria it appeared from observation and from panel data (Marshall and Merry, 1989), that the commitment to the principle of cautioning varied between divisions, and, according to probation staff, between individual police officers.

The project employed four part-time 'reparation workers', one for each division; they were probation service assistants, and were meant to investigate the possibilities of reparation in cases referred to them by the probation officer who attended the panel or from the panels themselves. There were important differences between the four areas, both in the working of the panels and (associated with these) in the practice of reparation. However, some features were common to all four panels. Most importantly, the panels were, in the opinion of their members and on the basis of observation, clearly dominated by the police, who, as well as chairing the meetings (which were held in the police divisional headquarters), controlled both the formal and the 'hidden' agenda, and effectively restricted the scope of cautioning to their own relatively modest conception of what was feasible.

The police line was pragmatic: cautions were a useful means of dealing with trivial cases quickly and efficiently, but there were tight limits to their applicability. Thus it was comparatively rare for a juvenile to be cautioned more than twice, or to be cautioned after a conviction.

It seems clear from the research (for a full statistical breakdown, see Marshall and Merry, 1989) that the reparation project was at best a marginal influence in the direction of diversion. This was the general feeling among the probation staff themselves. While the project probably did divert a few 'top end' juveniles, it may also have led to 'mesh-thinning' (Cohen, 1985) at the bottom end, when juveniles who in the absence of the opportunity for reparation would simply have been cautioned were expected additionally to undertake some reparative task. The worry felt by probation officers that this might happen was confirmed when the police began to list some cases on the panels' agenda as suitable for 'caution plus reparation'. This might of course have been a welcome development if the project's aim had been primarily to serve the interests of victims, but it is clear that there is no sense in which the project provided a general service to victims.

The experience of victims and offenders

Levels of satisfaction were higher among the offenders interviewed than among the victims. Just under half of the victims from the South and North divisions (ten out of twenty-three) expressed satisfaction with the project, but six out of seven from the West gave positive accounts, and only one (out of three) from the East was unhappy with the experience. In all a total of fifteen dissatisfied victims were interviewed. With such a small number it is hardly useful to quantify the reasons for the victims' dissatisfaction, and in any case several reasons were often given. Eight felt dissatisfied mainly because their expectations of compensation had been raised unrealistically, usually by the police officers in the case; others resented being asked to go through the process for the offender's benefit, or felt that the offender's attitude had been cynical or self-serving. A few felt perplexed when they met or received reparation from only one or two out of a number of offenders: they had the feeling that 'the ring-leader was getting away with it', or that they wanted to 'see the organ-grinder, not the monkey'. Offenders, and more particularly their parents, had similar feelings of injustice in such situations, which could arise from the panel's decision that reparation was not appropriate, on 'tariff' grounds, for every member of a group of joint offenders; some might be prosecuted, others cautioned without the expectation of reparation.

The accounts given by the seventeen victims who expressed some degree of satisfaction similarly conveyed a range of reasons, often in some combination. They were sometimes glad enough to have received some compensation, though for most of them this was a side-issue, and the payment of money was valued not for its financial worth (losses had often been covered by insurance anyway) but as a sign that the offender was genuinely sorry and concerned to make some amends. The most common motive among satisfied victims (expressed in some form by thirteen of the sample) was, however, a sense of social concern. They did not generally have unresolved feelings of anger towards the offender, but saw the project as providing an opportunity to do something useful and educative. The general sense of social responsibiliiity felt by these victims was heightened in some cases by an imaginative sympathy with the offender and by a feeling that 'it could have been my own son (or daughter)'. Two victims interviewed had children who had themselves been convicted of offences, and they were willing to do what they could to help other people's children to avoid a similar fate.

A primarily educational motive need not mean in all cases that the victim–offender meeting is a cool, unemotional affair; some victims' feelings were strongly engaged: a number managed not to deliver a moralising lecture, while other victims did use the meeting in this way, as emerged from their own accounts and from those of offenders. While it is doubtful if offenders derived any benefit from such a lecture, its value for the victims might easily be too quickly dismissed. One of the effects of victimisation is a sense of powerlessness, and to allow adult victims to become involved in the education of an offender may be a useful way of re-empowering them and helping to dispel the image they may have of the offender as a powerful and threatening force.

There were victims, however, who had a more personal stake in some resolution of the offence, however trivial. This could arise from a feeling that their status in relation to the offender needed to be re-affirmed. An example is the position of a teacher victimised by a pupil. A school is a tightly knit community in terms of the social consequences of offending – labelling for the offender and the threat to the status and professional credibility of the teacher. Both sides may therefore have a stake in the resolution of an offence, as we found in several cases in which there were certainly clear benefits for the teachers involved. There may be benefits for the children too: in one case, however, the teacher had been the tenth (and last) of a series of victims to whom the child had to apologise and repay money in the course of what must have been an arduous evening. The boy's offence had been to ask people in his village, including his teacher, to sponsor him at 50 pence a time for a non-existent charity event. Some reparative experiences in the North division, where this case comes from, were, on purpose, overtly punitive. As in some of the institutional reparations in Northamptonshire, offenders sometimes regarded them as unnecessarily punitive. For instance, a 13-year-old girl who had stolen from a schoolmate was asked to apologise to the victim, to pay compensation and to spend a day sweeping up leaves (North division, which produced the highest proportion of punitive-seeming settlements). The researcher stopped the interview when the girl began to cry as she spoke of the experience of sweeping up the leaves. Offenders and (especially) their parents were, however, often prepared to regard even quite strenuous reparative tasks as appropriate, and certainly as preferable to going to court. This applied mainly to indirect reparation: understandably parents were often very relieved that their children were not prosecuted.

Overall, thirty-six out of the forty-five offenders seen gave a generally positive account of their experience of reparation. The main sources of dissatisfaction of the other nine were a feeling that the reparative task they were asked to undertake was excessive; that the meeting had been no more than a meaningless 'going through the motions' (in these cases any suspicion the victim had of the offender's motives would have been well founded); and that injustice was inherent in the process since not all those involved in an offence were required to make reparation.

Conclusions

Our studies provide some useful insights into the problems of victim–offender reparation and mediation. Firstly, we think it should be stressed that victims do not always gain (nor do they always want to) from a punitive form of reparation given reluctantly by a grudging offender who feels coerced into meeting them. Indeed this may only add insult to the injury, sometimes in a literal sense. The process seems to work best when some form of symbolic exchange takes place, on grounds well prepared beforehand by social workers. The process can be very complex, and it requires a high level of skill to bring parties together effectively: it is also time-consuming; in South Yorkshire (a court-based scheme) it often took the full three weeks of the remand period to prepare and arrange a meeting (Smith *et al*, 1988).

Offenders seemed to benefit most from situations in which the human, rather than just material, cost of their crime could be shown to them; while victims, for their part, welcomed an apology that seemed voluntary and genuine. The South Yorkshire experience, only briefly alluded to here, reveals (and here it confirms the experience of other court-based schemes examined in Marshall and Merry, 1989) that mediation is achievable even within the judicial system. We see more scope for symbolic forms of reparation and mediation within social work practice than for some of the highly punitive restitutory models currently being debated in the USA (see Blagg, 1986).

If this is to be achieved then the model of practice offered within the Cumbria scheme should be viewed with some reservations. We have shown that there are contradictions between the aims of diversion and reparation. The Corby scheme appeared to have been more successful because it saw the two as distinct processes. Thus while, even in the Cumbria context, there were instances of productive meetings between victims and offenders and of various kinds of reparation which seemed satisfactory to both parties, our analysis of the project does tend to support the conclusions of Davis *et al* (1988) about the problems of attempting to use reparation in the service of diversion. Having said that, we want to reiterate that the willingness of the victims to take part in the project in the interests of the offenders counts as a real, and not a trivial motive; participation on this basis may be valuable to victims not just as a means of expressing a sense of social concern and resonsibility but as a way of recovering from the sense of helplessness and damaged status which victimisation may entail. We want also to make it clear that the probation staff associated with the project were fully alive to the contradictions witin which they worked, and were committed to a sensitive and intelligent practice within the limitations of the aims of the project. The lofty didactic tone of Davis and his colleagues, who find the current practice of reparation 'rather disappointing' (Davis *et al*, 1988, p 133), fails to recognise this self-awareness on the part of reparation workers; and when they write that 'many of the current attempts to promote "reparation" in this country are half-baked' (p 128) they seem to underestimate the difficulties of achieving a change of the kind which they – in common with many reparation workers – regard as desirable: towards a criminal justice system which would give a central place to reparative principles.

Conclusion

In this book we have tried to strike a balance. On the one hand we recognise that the context in which social work with offenders is practised in contemporary Britain is complex, difficult and often hostile. On the other hand, in describing and discussing recent trends and developments in social work thought and practice, we have tried to resist the still fashionable nihilism of 'nothing works'. Unlike many recent commentators on crime and criminal justice, we persist in thinking that social work has a valuable role to play in helping to resolve many of the personal and communal crises that are being left in the wake of the 'Thatcher revolution'. Like all revolutions, this one has had its predictable toll of casualties. We have suggested that social workers need to come to terms with the particular problems that working-class young people, both black and white, face in a society which seems to have no space or time for their demands, including even the most rudimentary demands for equality of access to public space. A society unequivocally bent upon the pursuit of personal gain and the glorification of all things that make a profit is hardly likely to put first the needs of those least likely to lubricate the wheels of the great financial gravy train. Social work, for all its undoubted shortcomings as a vehicle for social change, is still, for many who do not have the marketable skills necessary in this new Britain, one of the last sources of personal support. Young people in trouble and at risk are among the groups most in need of it.

The rhetoric of 'active citizenship', now being glibly canvassed by Conservative politicians as a panacea for contemporary alienation and social disruption, is in our view a cynical attempt to draw a veil over the real problems we, as a society, confront at present. Its appeal to good, worthy citizens to do a little for the 'unfortunate' amongst us (the 'deserving' ones, of course), conjures up a picture of our imagined past, when our forefathers built an empire abroad, and still had time to correct the moral habits of the fallen woman and discipline the parish waif. We are to remember, too, that our forefathers did this without payment, and without a diploma from the Central Council for Education and Training in Social Work. The Victorian era from which we are now encouraged to learn our values was also the era of what Foucault (1977) called 'the great incarceration'. Our ancestors' zeal for building empires, and gaining vicarious satisfaction from the sinful habits of the lower classes, was matched by their ingenuity in constructing vast institutions – which, naturally, they then proceeded to fill up.

The use, or, as everyone agrees, the over-use of custody which is the central feature of our penal system today suggests that there is at least one Victorian value which still commands support among those who have the power to make the crucial decisions. The prison crisis, which, we have argued, is more than just a crisis of overcrowding, is symptomatic of our inability to find rational and practical solutions to the problems of crime. There is simply no rational basis for the use of custody in many cases, which suggests that the fact that it is used may have as much or more to do with irrational fears about the social order in general as it has with changing behaviour of individual transgressors of the law. In particular, the criminalisation of black people in contemporary Britain is reflected in their over-representation within the court and prison populations. The social processes involved in bringing this about are, as we have suggested, complex and interacting; nevertheless, if our account of the centrality of racism in the ideology of 'Thatcher's Britain' is correct, one could see this incarceration of black people as a form of internal exile, some compensation for not being able to repatriate them to some place beyond the boundaries of the nation.

We have identified a number of ways in which the system of criminal justice discriminates against black people, from the policing of whole communities through to the practices of powerful state agencies and the courts. Although we do not discount the role instinctive prejudices play in this discriminatory process, we do not think that they provide an adequate explanation. What is entailed is the process of blaming the victims, a useful political manoeuvre which helps to account for the persistence of theories and images of black communities, families and individuals which portray them as different, deviant or incapable of adapting to some (usually ill-defined) notion of normality. In the case of people from an Asian background the problem may be less one of criminalisation than of indifference: a community which resists assimilation into the national community cannot hope to have the same claim upon time and efforts of police and other agencies, when it becomes the object of hostility. Moreover, although Asians are not believed to be individually predisposed towards crime, their presence in our society may itself be a crime, if they have entered the country illegally. Social work has shared the tendency to translate the problems of racism into a problem of 'their' inadequacies, although the strategies employed here may be more subtle and dressed up in opaque jargon: 'dysfunction', 'pathology', cultural impoverishment, and so on. The efforts recently made by, for example, Dominelli (1988) to work out in practical detail what an anti-racist practice might look like are important in showing how this tendency can be resisted; and so are the efforts of practitioners to subject their own and their agencies' practice to critical scrutiny.

We have discussed at some length the problems of demarcating groups in society on the basis of cultural differences. Cultural differences provide a convenient lens through which difficult and intractable problems, rooted in social processes, can be viewed as 'micro' issues and thereby made manageable, transformed into cases. But in so doing we create a neat divide between ourselves and the other culture, while conveniently side-stepping issues of oppression, racism, male sexuality, and so on. Social work's own baggage of professional 'theories' has not been free of this sort of evasiveness: it is a commonplace that there is a trace of conservative prejudices in the notions of pathological individuals, families and cultures which have played a central role in defining the agenda of social work practice since its infancy. It is ironic, then, that the New Right, in adopting the theme of culture, has turned it against social work itself. The 'culture of dependency', encouraging the poor to rely on the 'nanny-state', is alleged to be an inevitable consequence of misdirected support by social work agencies.

On the other hand, arguing that many problems are rooted in the social structure does not mean that they do not have individual effects on people. Practitioners never forget this, of course, and they are right to be irritated by academic critics who do, or who treat it as too obvious to mention. While we have tried to argue for forms of social and youth work practice which are sensitive to the official systems and wider social structures which inevitably impinge upon what happens when worker and client meet, we have also stressed the importance of face-to-face work. We think this a necessary and crucial part of social work practice, a complement to any work dealing with the system as a totality. We have, therefore, been critical of tendencies to reshape the role of social work into a systems management exercise, though we understand the pressures pushing in this direction. It is not only that this provides an escape route from the difficult, often thankless, sometimes despairing, work of dealing with clients; it also allows social work to aspire to the status of accountancy, producing facts and figures which, with luck, may convince the monetarist paymasters that the agency is an efficient, cost-effective enterprise.

There is a further range of issues which is currently being forced onto the agenda of social work, and of other agencies as well. Social workers practising in the criminal justice field have always had to confront, and try to answer, the question: 'Whose side are we on?' But the answers, never easy, are becoming harder to find, partly because of the opening-out of new areas for critical study which we noted as among the major achievements of recent criminology. There are several 'sides', and the choices are complex: do we side with the 'man on his knees', or with the women and children beneath his feet? It is no longer possible to ignore – it seems impossible that it was ever ignored – the reality of the oppression of women and children within the family and the community. As we become fully aware of this, it becomes urgent to deconstruct our images of families and communities as internally unified structures, based upon shared class relationships or ties of neighbourhood. Instead we have to be aware of the very real violence and abuse which arise as a result of power relationships based upon gender and age.

Again, this will not be news to social workers; but it seems clear that the Cleveland crisis in particular has radically changed the ways in which social work with families can be understood. In work with offenders, too, while the issues of gender and age have been added to the agenda by feminist writers, the enterprise has been advanced by women social workers, as they have struggled to find space within agency practice for work with girls and women, when the system is largely obsessed by the need to treat, or more often to control or punish, disorderly males. Some of the initaitives we mentioned in the social crime prevention field, which we suggested had more to do with youth social work than with crime prevention as such, were explicitly aimed at work with those groups of young people, such as girls and black youth, who have traditionally been marginal to the interests of mainstream youth provision. Such redrawing of the boundaries, in line with the shifts in criminology which we outlined, is essential if social and youth work are to challenge rather than merely reflect the dominant definitions of the problems of crime and youth.

Throughout the book we have argued for a nuanced treatment of the crime issue which is sensitive to the contradictory shifts in priorities which influence the criminal justice field. It would be a crude oversimplification of this process if one were to establish too forcefully some overall 'master-pattern' or plan, advocating either reform or repression and control. Once more, the arguments do not present themselves as neatly as might be hoped. For instance, those (and we count ourselves in this group) who have argued for more informality in the resolution of conflicts, and for the decarceration of offenders back into communities, may also want to argue for the increased criminalisation of certain forms of crime – for example, violence within the family, child abuse and racist attacks. While we have viewed sympathetically the efforts by social workers to introduce more informal and less bureaucratic responses to offending, we do not subscribe to the view that all of our problems stem from the intervention of the state, and if it went away, everything would be conflict-free. There are real structures of oppression within communities and families that can only be resolved by outside intervention; what we have tried to question is the way in which certain issues have been given priority and dealt with in ways which frequently leave these repressions unresolved and even intensified.

For those social workers most directly engaged in work within the criminal justice system, there are further complexities with which to grapple. It is clear that work with offenders is being increasingly conditioned by demands for tighter supervision and surveillance, for 'punishment in the community'; but, in discussing recent Government proposals on this issue, we suggested that there were contradictory elements which indicated that there is still room for some optimism. The proposals contain nuggets of good sense, which reveal the influence of liberal reformers, and, more importantly, the influence of practice. It is not much of an exaggeration to say that the proposals which are most feasible and potentially useful are those which derive most directly from what social workers have actually been doing; although practitioners may not entirely welcome the idea, and are likely to be surprised by it, it is plain that someone 'up there' has been looking and listening. We have tried to suggest what values and concepts might be most helpful in the response of social workers to the Government's proposals: while it is difficult, given the history of social work, to argue that punishment in the community is essentially alien to its traditions, it is still possible, and necessary, to establish preferences between forms of practice. We think that it does matter what you do when face to face with the clients, and have tried to support forms of work which do not entail any assumptions about the clients' pathology, which treat the clients as rational, and are open, participative, and relevant to the clients' self-defined problems.

The developments we have described in the field of reparation and mediation illustrate the interests many social workers have felt in moving away from the constrictions and limitations of the criminal justice system, and in developing ways of resolving some crime problems in a more informal setting, and by means that are more in line with social work's skills and concerns. Here social workers have also been responding to demands that they should be more concerned with the victims of crime. But the established priorities of the formal system are not easily overturned. The problems we identified in our research show that the system still exerts a powerful influence on the way informal justice operates. In practice, the process is still largely directed at the offender. Moreover, the outcomes of 'executive' justice, supposedly an informal, diversionary alternative to the formal system, can be as humiliating, punitive and stigmatising as anything a court would have imposed. A more radical shift, of the kind which provoked Enoch Powell to prophecies of anarchy, and which would entail a real transfer of power from the formal system to the people actually affected by the offence, is needed if the dominant assumptions about crime, offenders and victims are to be seriously challenged.

The emergence of multi-agency work gives a further twist to the chain of developments. We have argued that it is essential for social workers to become involved, in a critical way, in multi-agency bodies. The opportunity it offers is for social workers to exercise some influence on important areas of decision-making that can have real consequences and outcomes for clients. On the other hand, we have suggested that social workers need to resist being used to sanction the behaviour of other, more powerful, agencies; and they should certainly resist the temptation to see outcomes as successful in terms of improved liaison alone. The field of crime prevention offers illustrations of the way the crime issue can intensify problems in communities by taking too simplified a view of crime, and presenting the remedy in terms of techonlogy – nuts and bolts, entryphones and alarms, strengthened glass and climb-resistant paint. It also reveals the problems inherent in multi-agency work 'from above' which is not sensitive to the needs and problems of all the sections of communities, only to those of its recognised representatives But if crime prevention is to have a social as well as a 'situational' dimension, as we think it must, then social work and allied agencies need to be involved in local crime prevention initiatives; the social dimension will not come from anywhere else.

We hope to have shown that while the role and tasks of social work have changed in the last twenty years it still has an important and distinctive place in relation to crime and criminal justice. We remain optimistic that the core values which have traditionally been associated with social work will continue to inform, even on the margins, the official response to crime and crime problems. We have in mind values such as concern and respect for persons, support for the weak and vulnerable, and hope in people's capacity to grow and change. It is not easy in the present social and political context to retain these value; it is not even easy to express them without feeling an embarrassing sense of anachronism. But unless social work can continue to find a practical expression of such values our criminal justice system will become more repressive and discriminatory, and still less capable of delivering justice and fairness.

Bibliography

Advisory Council on the Treatment of Offenders (1963) *The Organisation of After-Care*. London: HMSO.

Anderson, B (1983) *Imagined Communities*. London: Verso.

Association for Juvenile Justice (AJJ) (1989) *Submission to the Home Office on the Green Paper*. London: AJJ.

Barker, M (1981) *The New Racism*. London: Junction Books.

Becker, H S (1963) *Outsiders*. New York: Free Press.

Bennett, T and Wright, R (1985) *Burglars on Burglary*. Aldershot: Gower.

Berman, M (1981) *All That Is Solid Melts into Air*. London: Verso.

Blagg, H (1985) Reparation and justice for juveniles. *British Journal of Criminology* 25: 267–79.

Blagg, H (1986) Punishment and restitution (review article). *British Journal of Criminology* 26: 303–6.

Blagg, H, Pearson, G, Sampson, A, Smith, D and Stubbs, P. (1988) Inter-aency co-ordination: rhetoric and reality. In Hope, T and Shaw M (eds) *Communities and Crime Reduction*. London: HMSO.

Blagg, H and Stubbs, P (1988) A child-centred practice? Multi-agency approaches to child sexual abuse. *Practice* 1: 2.

Borkowski, M, Murch, M and Walker, V (1983) *Marital Violence: The Community Response*. London: Tavistock.

Bottomley, K and Pease, K (1986) *Crime and Punishment: Interpreting the Data*. Milton Keynes: Open University.

Bottoms, A E (1974) On the decriminalisation of the English juvenile court. In Hood, R (ed.) *Crime, Criminology and Public Policy*. London: Heinemann.

Bottoms, A E (1977) Reflections on the renaissance of dangerousness. *Howard Journal* 16: 70–97.

Bottoms, A E (1981) The suspended sentence in England, 1967–1978. *British Journal of Criminology* 21: 1–26.

Bottoms, A E and McWilliams, W (1979) A non-treatment paradigm for probation practice. *British Journal of Social Work* 9 (2): 159–202.

Bottoms, A E and Stelman, A (1988) *Social Inquiry Reports*. London: Wildwood House/Community Care.

Box, S (1981) *Deviance, Reality and Society* (2nd ed). London: Holt, Rinehart and Winston.

Box, S (1987) *Recession, Crime and Punishment*. London: Macmillan.

Bridges, L (1983) Policing the urban wasteland. *Race and Class* 15: 13-30.

Brittan, L (1984) Speech to the Holborn Law Society, 14 March.

Bullock, W F and Tildesley, W M S (1984) *Special Requirements in Probation or Supervision Orders; A Local Case Study*. Cambridge: Institute of Criminology.

Campbell, B (1988) *Unofficial Secrets: Child Sexual Abuse – The Cleveland Case*. London: Virago.

Carlen, P (1983) *Women's Imprisonment: a Study in Social Control*. London: Routledge.

Centre on Youth, Crime and Community (1984) *Diversion: Corporate Action with Juveniles*. Lancaster: Centre of Youth, Crime and Community.

Children's Society (1989) *Response to the Home Office Green Paper on Punishment and Custody in the Community*. London: The Children's Society.

Children's Society Advisory Committee (1988) *Penal Custody for Juveniles – The Line of Least Resistance*. London: The Children's Society.

Christian, L (1983) *Policing by Coercion*. London: GLC Police Committee Support Unit.

Christie, N (1977) Conflicts as property. *British Journal of Criminology* 17: 1-15.

Clarke, J, Langan, M and Lee, P (1980) Social work: the conditions of crisis. In Carlen, P and Collison, M (eds.) *Radical Issues in Criminology*. London: Martin Robertson.

Clarke, R V G and Hough, M (1984) *Crime and Police Effectiveness*. London: HMSO.

Cohen, E (1987) Changing the domestic violence responses of urban police departments. *Responses* 10 (4): 20-25.

Cohen, P (1979) Policing the working class city. in NDC/CSE (eds) *Capitalism and the Rule of Law*. London: Hutchinson.

Cohen, S (1973) *Folk Devils and Moral Panics*. London: MacGibbon and Kee.

Cohen, S (1985) *Visions of Social Control*. Cambridge: Polity Press.

Community Development Projects (1977) *Gilding the Ghetto*. London: Home Office.

Cooper, E (1987) Probation practice in the criminal and civil courts. In Harding, J (ed) *Probation and the Community*. London: Tavistock.

Cornish, D B and Clarke, R V G (1975) *Residential Treatment and its Effects on Delinquency*. London: HMSO.

Cornish, D B and Clarke, R V G (eds) (1986) *The Reasoning Criminal*. Berlin: Springer-Verlag.

Corrigan, P (1979) *Schooling the Smash Street Kids*. London: Macmillan.

Crow, I (1987) Black people and criminal justice in the UK. *Howard Journal of Criminal Justice* 26 (4): 303-14.

Davies, M (1969) *Probationers in their Social Environment*. London: HMSO.

Davies, M (1974a) *Social Work in the Environment*. London: HMSO.

Davies, M (1974b) *Prisoners of Society*. London: Routledge and Kegan Paul.

Davies, M (1982) Community based alternatives to custody: the right place for the probation service. Address to a conference of Chief Probation Officers (unpublished).

Davis, G, Boucherat, J and Watson, D (1988) Reparation in the service of diversion: the subordination of a good idea. *Howard Journal of Criminal Justice* **27**: 127–34.

Davis, M (1985) Urban renaissance and the spirit of post-modernism. *New Left Review* **151**.

Denman, G (1982) *Intensive Intermediate Treatment with Juvenile Offenders: A Handbook of Assessment and Groupwork Practice*. Lancaster: Centre of Youth, Crime and Community.

DHSS (1987) *Reports to Courts: Practice Guidance for Social Workers*. London: HMSO.

Ditchfield, J A (1976) *Police Cautioning in England and Wales*. London: HMSO.

Dobash, R E and Dobash, R P (1979) *Violence Against Wives: A Case Against the Patriarchy*. London: Open Books.

Dominelli, L (1984) Differential justice: domestic labour, community service and female offenders. *Probation Journal* **31** (3): 100–4.

Dominelli, L (1988) *Anti Racist Social Work*. London: Macmillan.

Donzelot, J (1980) *The Policing of Families*. London: Hutchinson.

Downes, D (1983) *Law and Order: Theft of an Issue?* London: Fabian Society/Cobden Trust.

Downes, D (1988) The sociology of crime and social control inBritain 1950–1987. *British Journal of Criminology* **28** (2) (Special issue): 45–57.

Downs, D and Rock, P (1988) *Understanding Deviance* (2nd ed). Oxford: University Press.

Drakeford, M (1983) Probation: containment or liberty? *Probation Journal* **30** (1): 7–10.

Dunlop, A (1974) *The Approved School Experience*. London: HMSO.

Dunning, E G, Murphy, P J and Williams, J (1987) *The Roots of Football Hooliganism: an Historical and Sociological Study*. London: Routledge.

Eaton, M (1986) *Justice for Women?* Milton Keynes: Open University.

Ennew, J (1986) *The Sexual Exploitation of Children*. Cambridge: Polity Press.

Fairhead, S (1981) *Day Centres and Probation*. London: HMSO.

Faragher, T (1985) The police response to violence against women in the home. In Pahl, J (ed) *Private Violence and Public Policy*. London: Routledge.

Farrington, D P (1981) The Lifetime prevalence of convictions. *British Journal of Criminology* **21**: 173–5.

Farrington, D P and Bennett, T (1981) Police cautioning of juveniles in London. *British Journal of Criminology* **21**: 123–35.

Farrington, D P and Morris, A (1983) Sex, sentencing and reconviction. *British Journal of Criminology* **23**: 229–48.

Feest, J (1988) *Reducing the Prison Population: Lessons from the West German Experience*. London: NACRO.

Fine, B and Millar, R (eds) (1986) *Policing the Miners' Strike*. London: Lawrence and Wishart.

Fishbein, M and Ajzen, I (1975) *Belief, Attitude and Intention: An Introduction to Theory and Research*. Reading, Massachusetts: Addison-Wesley.

Fitzgerald, M and Sim, J (1982) *British Prisons* (2nd ed). Oxford: Blackwell.

Folkard, M S, Smith, D E and Smith, D D (1979) *IMPACT Vol II*. London: HMSO.

Foren, R and Bailey, R (1968) *Authority in Social Casework*. Oxford: Pergamon.

Forrester, M, Chatterton, M and Pease, K (1988) *The Kirkholt Burglary Prevention Project*. London: Home Office.

Foucault, M (1977) *Discipline and Punish*. London: Allen Lane.

Gifford, Lord (1986) *The Broadwater Farm Inquiry*. London: Karia.

Gill, K (1988) The way ahead (Conference address). Glasgow: IT Resource Centre.

Giller, H and Tutt, W (1987) Police cautioning: the continuing practice of diversity. *Criminal Law Review*: 367–74.

Gilroy, P (1987) *There Ain't No Black in the Union Jack*. London: Hutchinson.

Gilroy, P and Sim, J (1985) Law, order and the state of the left. *Capital and Class* **25**: 15–55.

Glaser, D and Frosh, S (1988) *Child Sexual Abuse*. London: Macmillan.

Gordon, P (1984) Community policing: towards the local police state? *Critical Social Policy***10**: 39–58.

Gramsci, A (1971) *Prison Notebooks*. London: Lawrence and Wishart.

Greater Manchester NAPO Branch Executive (1988) Tackling offending: a reaction plan? *Probation Journal* **35**: (4): 137–9.

Gregory, D and Urry, J (eds) (1985) *Social Relations and Spatial Structures*. London: Macmillan.

Hall, S (1980) *Drifting into a Law and Order Society*. London: Cobden Trust.

Hall, S, Clarke, J, Critcher, C, Jefferson, T and Roberts, B (1978) *Policing the Crisis*. London: Macmillan.

Harding, J (ed) (1987) *Probation and the Community*. London: Tavistock.

Harris, R and Webb, D (1987) *Welfare, Power and Juvenile Justice*. London: Tavistock.

Harvey, L and Pease, K (1988) Custodial careers in the UK. In Harrison, A and Gretton, J (eds) *Crime UK 1988*. Newbury: Policy Journals.

Heal, K, Tarling, R and Burrows, J (1985) Introduction. In Heal, Tarling and Burrows (eds) *Policing Today*. London: HMSO.

Heidensohn, F (1985) *Women and Crime*. London: Macmillan.

Heidensohn, F (1988) *Crime and Society*. London: Macmillan

Hinks, N and Smith, G (1985) Diversion in practice. *Probation Journal* **32**: 48–50.

Hirschi, T (1969) *Causes of Delinquency*. Berkeley: University of California Press.

Holdaway, S (1986) Police and social work relations: problems and possibilities. *British Journal of Social Work* **16**: 137–60.

Home Office (1979) *Report of the Committee of Inquiry into the United Kingdom Prison Services*. London: HMSO.

Home Office (1980) *Young Offenders* (Cmnd 8045). London: HMSO.

Home Office (1984) *Statement of National Objectives and Priorities*. London: Home Office.

Home Office (1988a) *Criminal Statistics for England and Wales 1987*. London: HMSO.

Home Office (1988b) *Punishment, Custody and the Community*. London: HMSO.

Home Office (1988c) *Tackling Offending: An Action Plan*. London: Home Office.

Hooper, C (1988) Getting him off the hook. *Trouble and Strife*, November.

Hope, T (1985) *Implementing Crime Prevention Measures*. London: HMSO.

Hope, T and Shaw, M (eds) (1988) *Communities and Crime Reduction*. London: HMSO.

Hough, M (1985) Managing with less technology. In Heal, K, Tarling, R and Burrows, J (eds) *Policing Today*. London: HMSO.

Hough, M and Moxon D (1985) Dealing with offenders: popular opinion and the views of victims. *Howard Journal of Criminal Justice* **24**: 160–4.

Hudson, A (1988) Boys will be boys: masculinisation and the juvenile justice system. *Critical Social Policy* **21**: 30–48.

Hulsman, L (1977) The causes and manifestations of recent trends in juvenile delinquency. Paper to UN seminar on young offenders, Lillehamer.

IT Resource Centre (1986) *Review of IT in Scotland: Part 1*. Glasgow: ITRC.

Jepson, N and Elliot, K (1986) *Shared Working Between Prison and Probation Officers*. London: Home Office.

John, E (1986) *Youth Social Work*. Leicester: National Youth Bureau.

Jones, S (1986) *Policewomen and Equality*. London: Macmillan.

Jordan, B (1983) Criminal justice and probation in the 1980s. *Probation Journal* **30** (3): 83–8.

Juvenile Crime Section (NACRO) (1988) *Juvenile Cautioning: A Monitoring Guide*. London: NACRO.

Kelly, L (1988) *Surviving Sexual Violence*. Cambridge: Polity Press.

Kelly, L and Radford, J (1987) The problem of men: feminist perspectives on sexual violence. In Scraton, P (ed) *Law, Order and the Authoritarian State*. Milton Keynes: Open University Press.

Kilker, T (1988) The police response. Paper presented to the Longman's seminar, Child Sexual Abuse, Barbican Centre, London.

King, M (1988) *How to Make Social Crime Prevention Work: The French Experience*. London: NACRO.

Landau, S F and Nathan, G (1983) Selecting delinquents for cautioning in the London Metropolitan Area. *British Journal of Criminology* **23**: 128–49.

Laycock, G (1985) *Property marking: a deterrent to domestic burglary?* London: Home Office.

Laycock, G and Tarling, R (1985) Police force cautioning: policy and practice. *Howard Journal of Criminal Justice* **24** (2): 81–92.

Lea, J, Jones, T, Woodhouse, T and Young, J (1987) *Preventing Crime: The Hilldrop Project*. London: Middlesex Polytechnic.

Lea, J, Jones, T and Young, J (1986) *Saving the Inner City: Broadwater Farm – A Strategy for survival*. London: Middlesex Polytechnic.

Lea, J and Young, J (1982) The riots in Britain 1981: urban violence and political marginalisation. In Cowell, D (ed) *Policing the Riots*. London: Junction Books.

Lea, J and Young J (1984) *What is to be Done about Law and Order?* Harmondsworth: Penguin.

Levitas, R (ed) (1986) *The Ideology of the New Right*. Cambridge: Polity Press.

Loney, M (1980) Community action and anti-poverty strategies: some transatlantic comparisons. *Community Development Journal* **15**: 91–104.

McLoone, P, Oulds, G and Morris, J (1987) Alcohol education groups: compulsion v. voluntarism. *Probation Journal* **34** (1): 25.

Maguire, M (1982) *Burglary in a Dwelling.* London: Heinemann.

Maguire, M and Corbett, C (1987) *The Effects of Crime and the Work of Victim Support Schemes.* Aldershot: Gower.

Mair, G (1986) Ethnic minorities, probation and the magistrates' courts. *British Journal of Criminology* **26**: 147–55.

Marshall, T F (1984) *Reparation, Conciliation and Mediation.* London: Home Office.

Marshall, T F and Merry, S (1989) *Crime and Accountability: Victim/Offender Mediation in Practice.* London: Home Office (forthcoming).

Marshall, T F and Walpole, M (1985) *Bringing People Together.* London: Home Office.

Martin, F, Fox, S J and Murray, K (1981) *Children out of Court.* Edinburgh: Scottish Academic Press.

Martin, J P (1988) The development of criminology in Britain, 1948–1960. *British Journal of Criminology* **28** (2) (Special issue): 35–44.

Martinson, R (1974) What works? Questions and answers about penal reform. *The Public Interest* **10**: 22–54.

Matthews, R and Young, J (eds) (1986) *Confronting Crime.* London: Sage.

Matza, D (1964) *Delinquency and Drift.* New York: John Wiley.

Maynard, M (1985) The response of social workers to domestic violence. In Pahl, J (ed) *Private Violence and Public Policy.* London: Routledge.

Mays, J B (1954) *Growing up in the City.* Liverpool: Liverpool University Press.

Miller, A (1985) *Thou Shalt Not Be Aware: Society's Betrayal of the Child.* London: Virago.

Millham, S, Bullock, R and Cherrett, P (1975) *After Grace – Teeth.* London: Chaucer.

Morris, A and McIsaac, M (1978) *Juvenile Justice?* London: Heinemann.

Morris, A, Giller, H, Szwed, E and Geach, H (1980) *Justice for Children.* London: Macmillan.

Moxon, D (ed) (1985) *Managing Criminal Justice.* London: HMSO.

Moynihan, D P (1965) *The Negro Family: The Case for National Action.* Washington, DC: US Department of Labour.

NACRO (1986) *Black People and the Criminal Justice System.* London: NACRO.

NACRO (1988) *Diverting Juveniles from Custody: Findings from the Fourth Census of Projects Funded under the DHSS IT Initiative.* London: NACRO.

NAPO (1985) *Criminal Justice: An Alternative Strategy.* London: NAPO.

NAPO (1988) *Punishment, Custody and the Community: The Response of the National Association of Probation Officers.* London: NAPO.

Nelson, S (1986) *Incest: Fact and Myth.* Edinburgh: Strumillion.

Nuttall, C P (1988) Crime prevention in Canada. In Hope, T and Shaw, M (eds) *Communities and Crime Reduction.* London: HMSO.

Nuttall, C P *et al* (1977) *Parole in England and Wales.* London: HMSO.

Pahl, J (1985) (ed) *Private Violence and Public Policy.* London: Routledge.

Paley, J, Thomas, J and Norman, G (1986) *Rethinking Youth Social Work.* Leicester: National Youth Bureau.

Parker, H, Casburn, M and Turnbull, D (1981) *Receiving Juvenile Justice.* Oxford: Blackwell.

Parker, R and Williams B (1976) Probation officers and parole supervision. *Probation Journal* 23 (4): 112-6.

Pearson, G (1975) *The Deviant Imagination*. London: Macmillan.

Pearson, G (1983) *Hooligan: A History of Respectable Fears*. London: Macmillan.

Pearson, G, Sampson, A, Blagg, H, Stubbs, P and Smith D (1989) Policing racism. In Morgan, R and Smith, D J (eds) *Coming to Terms with Policing*. London: Routledge.

Pease, K (1983) Penal innovations. In Lishman, J (ed) *Research Highlights 5: Social Work with Adult Offenders*. Aberdeen: University of Aberdeen.

Pease, K (1984) A five year plan for probation research. In Senior, P (ed) *Probation: Direction, Innovation and Change in the 1980s*. London: NAPO.

Pease, K (1985a) The future of research and information in the probation service. In Sainsbury, E (ed), *Research and Information in the Probation Service*. Sheffield: University of Sheffield.

Pease, K (1985b) Community service orders. In Tonry, M H and Morris, N (eds) *Crime and Justice: An Annual Review of Research*. Chicago: University of Chicago Press.

Pease, K and McWilliams, W (1981) (eds) *Community Service by Order*. Edinburgh: Scottish Academic Press.

Pinder, R (1984) *Probation Work in a Multi-Racial Society: A Research Report*. Leeds: Applied Anthropology Group, Leeds University.

Pitts, J (1988) *The Politics of Juvenile Crime*. London: Sage.

Poulantzas, N (1978) *State, Power, Socialism*. London: Verso.

Powell, E (1985) Speech to Cambridge University Conservative Association, 20 October.

Pratt, J (1985) Delinquency as a scarce resource. *Howard Journal of Criminal Justice* 24 (2): 81-92.

Pratt, J (1986) Diversion from the juvenile court. *British Journal of Criminology* 26 (3): 212-33.

Pratt, J (1987) A revisionist history of intermediate treatment. *British Journal of Social Work* 17: 417-36.

Priestley, P *et al* (1977) *Social Skills and Personal Problem-Solving: A Handbook of Methods*. London: Routledge and Kegan Paul.

Prison Service (1988) *Report on the Work of the Prison Service April 1987– March 1988* (Cmd 516). London: HMSO.

Rainwater, L (1978) *Behind Ghetto Walls*. Harmondsworth: Penguin.

Raynor, P (1978) Compulsory persuasion: a problem for correctional social work. *British Journal of Social Work* 8 (4): 411-24.

Raynor, P (1985) *Social Work, Justice and Control*. Oxford: Blackwell.

Raynor, P (1988) *Probation as an Alternative to Custody*. Aldershot: Gower.

Reiner, R (1985) *The Politics of the Police*. Brighton: Wheatsheaf.

Reiner, R and Shapland J (1987) Introduction: Why police? *British Journal of Criminology* 27 (1): 1-3.

Richardson, N (1988) *Justice by Geography II*. Manchester: Social Information Systems.

Riley, D and Tuck M (1986) The theory of reasoned action. In Cornish, D B and Clarke, R V G (eds), *The Reasoning Criminal*. Berlin: Springer-Verlag.

Rock, P (1986) *A View from the Shadows*. Oxford: University Press.

Rock, P (1988) The present state of criminology in Britain. *Brtish Journal of Criminology* **28** (2) (Special issue): 58–69.

Rose, G and Marshall, T F (1974) *Counselling and School Social Work*. London: John Wiley.

Rosenbaum, D P (1988) A critical eye on neighbourhood watch: does it reduce crime and fear? In Hope, T and Shaw, M (eds) *Communities and Crime Reduction*. London: HMSO.

Rutherford, A (1983) The Criminal Justice Act '82 and the use of probation. *Probation Journal* **30** (3): 93–5.

Rutherford, A (1984) *Prisons and the Process of Justice*. London: Heinemann.

Rutherford, A (1986) *Growing out of Crime*. Harmondsworth: Penguin.

Sampson, A, Stubbs, P, Smith, D, Pearson, G and Blagg, H (1988) Crime, localities and the multi-agency approach. *British Journal of Criminology* **28**: 478–93.

Saraga, E and Macleod, M (1987) Abuse of trust. *Marxism Today* (August): 10–13.

Scarman, Lord (1981) *The Brixton Disorders 10–12 April 1981* (Cmnd. 8427). London: HMSO.

Scraton, P (1985) *The State of the Police*. London: Pluto Press.

Scraton, P (ed) (1987) *Law, Order and the Authoritarian State*. Milton Keynes: Open University.

Scraton, P, Sim, J and Skidmore, P (1988) Through the barricades: prisoner protest and penal policy in Scotland. *Journal of Law and Society* **15** (3): 247–62.

Shapland, J (1984) Victims, the criminal justice system and compensation. *British Journal of Criminology* **24**: 131–49.

Shapland, J and Vagg, J (1987) Using the police. *British Journal of Criminology* **27**: 54–63.

Shaw, M (1974) *Social Work in Prison*. London: HMSO.

Sim, J, Scraton, P and Gordon, P (1987) Introduction: crime, the state and critical analysis. In Scraton, P (ed) *Law, Order and the Authoritarian State*. Milton Keynes: Open University Press.

Simpkin, M (1979) *Trapped within Welfare*. London: Macmillan.

Sinclair, I (1971) *Hostels for Probationers*. London: HMSO.

Smith, D (1984) Law and order: arguments for what? *Critical Social Policy* **11**: 33–45.

Smith, D (1987) The limits of positivism in social work research. *British Journal of Social Work* **17**: 401–16.

Smith, D and Blagg, H (1989) The Cumbrian reparation scheme. *British Journal of Social Work* August (forthcoming).

Smith, D, Blagg, H and Derricourt, N (1988) Mediation in South Yorkhire. *British Journal of Criminology* **28**: 378–95.

Smith, D I (1987) *Reshaping the Youth Service*. Leicester: NYB.

Smith, D J and Gray, J (1983) *Police and People in London*. London: Policy Studies Institute.

Southgate, P and Ekblom, P (1985) Contacts between police and public: findings from the British Crime Survey. In Heal, K, Tarling, R and Burrows, J (eds) *Policing Today*. London: HMSO.

Spencer, J (1988) Probation, the technology of power and the new politics. *Probation Journal* **35** (2): 52–4.

Stern, V (1987) *Bricks of Shame*. Harmondsworth: Penguin.

Stewart, G and Smith, D (1987) Help for children in custody: some implications of probation withdrawal. *British Journal of Criminology* 27: 302–10.

Stewart, G and Tutt, N (1987) *Children in Custody*. Aldershot: Avebury.

Strathclyde Regional Council (1987) *Working with Young People: Working Group Report on Young People at Risk*. Glasgow: Strathclyde Regional Council.

Stubbs, P (1988a) *The Reproduction of Racism in State Social Work*. PhD thesis, University of Bath.

Stubbs, P (1988b) Relationships with the police: intermediate treatment and the multi-agency approach. *Youth and Policy* 24: 16–19.

Tarling, R (1979) *Sentencing Practice in Magistrates' Courts*. London: HMSO.

Taylor, I (1981) *Law and Order: Arguments for Socialism*. London: Macmillan.

Taylor, I, Walton, P and Young, J (1973) *The New Criminology*. London: Routledge and Kegan Paul.

Taylor, I, Walton, P and Young J (eds) (1975) *Critical Criminology*. London: Routledge and Kegan Paul.

Thomas, J E (1972) *The English Prison Officer since 1850*. London: Routledge and Kegan Paul.

Thomas, J E and Pooley, R (1980) *The Exploding Prison*. London: Junction Books.

Thomas, T (1986) *The Police and Social Workers*. Aldershot: Gower.

Thorpe, D H, Smith, D, Green, C J and Paley, J H (1980) *Out of Care: The Community Support of Juvenile Offenders*. London: Allen and Unwin.

Trasler, G (1962) *The Explanation of Criminality*. London: Routledge and Kegan Paul.

Traux, R R and Carkhuff, C B (1967) *Towards Effective Counselling and Psychotherapy*. Chicago: Aldine.

Tutt, N and Giller, H (1983) Police cautioning of juveniles: the practice of diversity. *Criminal Law Review*: 587–95.

Tutt, N and Giller, H (1984) *Social Inquiry Reports* (audiotape). Lancaster: Information Systems, Lancaster.

Urry, J (1985) Social relations, space and time. In Gregory, D and Urry, J (eds) *Social Relations and Spatial Structures*. London: Macmillan.

Walker, M (1987) Note: the ethnic origin of prisoners. *British Journal of Criminology* 27: 202–6.

Waters, R (1988) Race and the criminal justice process: two empirical studies on social inquiry reports and ethnic minority defendants. *British Journal of Criminology* 28: 82–94.

Weatheritt, M (1986) *Innovations in Policing*. London: Croom Helm.

Webb, D (1984) More on gender and justice: girl offenders on supervision. *Sociology* 18: 3.

White, T (1988) In consideration of youth crime: an anti-custody strategy for young people. *Ajjust* 17: 12–16.

Willis, C (1985) The use, effectiveness and impact of police stop and search powers. In Heal, K, Tarling, R and Burrows, J (eds) *Policing Today*. London: HMSO.

Willis, P (1977) *Learning to Labour*. London: Saxon House.

Willis, P (1984) Youth Unemployment: 2. Ways of living. *New Society* 5 April: 13–15.

Wilson, J Q (1975) *Thinking About Crime*. New York: Basic Books.

Wilson, J Q and Kelling, G L (1982) Broken windows: the police and neighbourhood safety. *The Atlantic Monthly* March: 29–38.

Winnicott, C (1962) Casework and agency function. *Case Conference* 8: 178–84.

Wootton, B (1978) *Crime and Penal Policy*. London: Allen and Unwin.

Wright, M (1982) *Making Good*. London: Burnett Books.

Wright, P (1985) *On Living in an Old Country*. London: Verso.

Zehr, H (1985) *New Perspectives on Crime and Justice*. Valparaiso: MCC US Office of Criminal Justice.